D0246366

IMPROVE
YOUR
COMMUNICATION
SKILLS

CREATING SUCCESS

The best-selling series is back and better than ever

MARCH 2013

Because you only have one chance in life to make a good impression.

IMPROVE YOUR COMMUNICATION SKILLS

ALAN BARKER

CREATING SUCCESS

KoganPage

First published in 2000 by Kogan Page Limited
Second edition 2006
Revised second edition 2010
Third edition 2013
Reprinted 2013, 2014 (three times), 2015

2nd Floor, 45 Gee Street	1518 Walnut Street, Suite 1100	4737/23 Ansari Road
London EC1V 3RS	Philadelphia PA 19102	Daryaganj
United Kingdom	USA	New Delhi 110002
www.koganpage.com		India

© Alan Barker 2000, 2006, 2010, 2013

The right of Alan Barker to be identified as the author of this work has been asserted by him in accordance with the Copyright, Designs and Patents Act 1988.

ISBN   978 0 7494 6716 6
E-ISBN   978 0 7494 6717 3

British Library Cataloguing-in-Publication Data

A CIP record for this book is available from the British Library.

Library of Congress Cataloging-in-Publication Data

Barker, Alan, 1956-
   Improve your communication skills / Alan Barker. – 3rd Edition.
      pages cm
   ISBN 978-0-7494-6716-6 – ISBN (invalid) 978-0-7494-6717-3 (ebk.)   1. Business communication.   I. Title.
   HF5718.B365 2013
   651.7–dc23   2012045498

Typeset by Graphicraft Limited, Hong Kong
Printed and bound by CPI Group (UK) Ltd, Croydon, CR0 4YY

CONTENTS

About this book   viii

1   **What is communication?**   1

The transmission model   1
From transmission to reception: turing the model
round   3
Getting to know each other   8
A new definition of communication   12
In brief   13

2   **How conversations work**   14

The three basic rules of good conversation   15
Why do conversations go wrong?   23
Putting conversations in context   23
Working out the relationship   25
Managing behaviour   31
The uses of conversation   33
In brief   34

3   **Seven ways to improve your conversations**   35

Clarify your objective   36
Structure your thinking   38

Manage your time   48
Find common ground   51
Move beyond argument   52
Summarize often   57
Use visuals   59
In brief   62

4 The skills of enquiry   64

Paying attention   65
Treating the speaker as an equal   69
Cultivating ease   70
Encouraging   71
Asking quality questions   73
Rationing information   75
Giving positive feedback   76
In brief   79

5 The skills of persuasion   81

Character, logic and passion   81
What's the big idea?   84
Arranging your ideas   88
Expressing your ideas   91
Remembering your ideas   93
Delivering effectively   94
In brief   95

6 Making a presentation   98

Putting yourself on show   99
Preparing for the presentation   101
Managing the material   102
Controlling the audience   114

Looking after yourself   116
Answering questions   117
In brief   118

Putting it in writing   120

Writing for results   120
Making reading easier   121
Writing step by step   122
Designing the document   123
Writing a first draft   135
Effective editing   137
Writing for the web   144
In brief   150

Networking: the new conversation   152

To network or not to network?   153
Preparing to network   155
The skills of networking conversations   166
Following up and building your network   173
In brief   181

Appendix: where to go from here   183

ABOUT THIS BOOK

Effective communication is central to business success.

Survey after survey shows that being able to communicate well makes a critical difference at work – and that too many of us aren't up to the mark. The National Association of Colleges and Employers, in their 2011 Job Outlook Report, found that employers listed verbal communication skills as the number one soft skill they sought in new employees. According to another survey that same year, by the American Management Association, more than half of executives said their employees were only average in communication skills.

Why do these skills matter so much? Partly because we're no longer working in simple command and control structures. In these days of project and matrix management, we need to be able to influence each other without wielding managerial authority. In an era of outsourcing and networking, our success depends on building effective relationships with customers, suppliers and business partners. Effective communication means leaping the barriers that divide specialisms, departments and corporate cultures.

The new technologies are having a huge effect. We need to be able to adapt our style to the needs of different channels: to the telephone and the videoconference, to email and texting and the demands of social media. It's not just the boundaries between different professions that are breaking down; the distinction between corporate communication and social gossip is becoming fuzzy – some might say, dangerously so. Above all, electronic media are shifting the relationship between writing and speaking. Work, along with the rest of life, is becoming more and more of a conversation – and often a conversation that's written down.

Conversation is the oldest form of human communication, and increasingly the most up-to-date. The more flexible our conversation skills, the more effective will be our meetings, customer relationships and presentations. Even our reports, our emails and our texts will benefit. Conversation is at the heart of effective business communication.

How can we begin to improve the quality of our conversations at work? This book seeks to answer that question.

WHAT IS COMMUNICATION?

How would you define the word 'communication'? It's a question I often ask at the start of training courses. After a little thought, people often come up with a sentence like this.

> Communication is the act of transmitting information effectively.

We seem to take this definition for granted. But just how accurate is it?

THE TRANSMISSION MODEL

That word 'transmitting' suggests that we tend to think of communication as a technical process. And the history of the word 'communication' supports this idea.

In the nineteenth century, the word 'communication' referred mainly to the movement of goods and people. We still use the word like this, of course: roads and railways are forms of communication, just as much as speaking or writing. And we still use the images of the industrial revolution – the canal, the railway and the postal service – as metaphors for communication. Information, like freight, comes in 'bits'; it needs to be stored, transferred and retrieved. And we describe the movement of information in terms of a 'channel', along which information 'flows'.

This transport metaphor readily adapted itself to the new, electronic technologies of the twentieth century. We talk about 'telephone lines' and 'television channels'. Electronic information comes in 'bits', stored in 'files' or 'vaults'. The words 'download' and 'upload' use the freight metaphor; email uses postal imagery.

And we apply the transmission metaphor to human communication. We 'have' an idea (as if it were an object). We 'put the idea into words' (like putting it into a box); we try to 'put our idea across' (by pushing it or 'conveying' it); and the 'receiver' – hopefully – 'gets' the idea. We may need to 'unpack' the idea before the receiver can 'grasp' it. Of course, we need to be careful to avoid 'information overload'.

The transmission model is certainly attractive. It gives the impression that information is objective and quantifiable: something that you and I will always understand in exactly the same way. It makes communication seem measurable, predictable and consistent: sending an email seems to be evidence that I've communicated to you. Above all, the model is simple: we can draw a diagram to illustrate it.

But does the transmission model reflect what actually happens when people communicate? And, if it's so easy to understand information, why does communication – especially in organizations – so often go wrong?

Wiio's Laws

Communication in organizations is notoriously unreliable. Otto Wiio (born 1928) is a Finnish professor of human communication. He's best known for a set of humorous maxims about how inaccurate the transmission model of communication is.

Communication usually fails, except by accident.

If communication can fail, it will fail.

If communication cannot fail, it still usually fails.

If communication seems to succeed in the way you intend – someone's misunderstood.

If you are content with your message, communication is certainly failing.

If a message can be interpreted in several ways, it will be interpreted in a manner that maximizes the damage.

There is always someone who knows better than you what your message means.

The more we communicate, the more communication fails.

Despite Professor Wiio's amusing insights into the inadequacy of the transmission model, we rarely question it. We rarely ask whether we might be missing something in our attempts to communicate more effectively.

FROM TRANSMISSION TO RECEPTION: TURNING THE MODEL ROUND

So what *is* wrong with the transmission model? Well, to begin with, a message differs from a parcel in a very obvious way. When

I send the parcel, I no longer have it; when I send a message, I still have it. But there's a more serious reason why the model fails to describe communication accurately.

The model is the wrong way round.

Here's the first and most important point to make about communication.

> Communication begins, not with transmission, but with reception.

No matter how effectively I transmit information, it won't communicate to you if you don't receive it. And in order to receive it, you have to do three things.

- You have to pay attention.
- You have to understand.
- You have to put what you understand in context.

Paying attention

Whatever you notice has the potential to communicate with you.

- If you notice the sign warning of a bend in the road, you can make use of it.
- If you notice the loud siren that suddenly blares through the office, you can respond to it.
- If you notice me gesturing wildly at you across a crowded room, you can make yourself ready to understand the message I'm trying to communicate.

In all three of these instances, your attention is being deliberately grabbed. The sign is positioned where you can see it at the side of the road; it's large and brightly coloured. The siren is loud and sudden, in order to attract your attention to a potential emergency. I make my gestures big, energetic and unusual so that your attention will be drawn to them.

But of course, we often notice things that are not intended to communicate to us. We notice the rabbit running out in front of the car, or our colleagues leaping out of their chairs as the siren rings, or the people staring oddly at the strange man pretending to be a windmill in the corner of the bar. All of these things have the potential to communicate *if we notice them*.

Communication begins when we start paying attention.

How we understand

Of course, paying attention isn't sufficient for communication to happen. We also need to *understand* what we're looking at. So how do we do that?

Essentially, understanding is a *pattern-matching* process. We create meaning by matching external stimuli from our environment to mental patterns inside our brains.

Let's look at those three examples again.

- That sign on the road would mean nothing to you if you didn't have a mental pattern of that sign already in your head. You learnt that sign, either by reading a manual or by asking people around you. You understand the sign because you can match it to a mental model.

- Similarly, you know that sudden loud sounds usually signal danger. In this case, the mental model is probably imprinted genetically in your brain: all hearing animals will react violently to sudden, loud sounds.

- And those wild gestures I'm making across the room also trigger mental patterns: you've learnt that these movements mean 'pay attention, something important's happening over here!'

Understanding, then, is an active process. We always participate in the process by providing the mental patterns that tell us what the information might mean.

Sometimes, the mental pattern-matching is simple. That road sign, for example, is designed to deliver a clear message. But very often, we're working with information that's incomplete, garbled or ambiguous. And on those occasions, we have to fill in the gaps.

For example, take a look at this image.

Figure 1.1 A Kanizsa triangle

You can almost certainly see a white triangle here. Of course, there is no white triangle; your brain has matched the available information to the mental patterns it has stored up, and come up with the best guess of a white triangle. (The triangle is named after Gaetano Kanizsa, an Italian psychologist and artist, founder of the Institute of Psychology of Trieste.)

This process of filling in the gaps is called 'perceptual completion', and it's not limited to visual information. Perceptual completion shows that *everything* we understand is a best guess of what's there.

Putting it all in context

Because all understanding is a best guess, most of us have become very good at guessing what information means.

The key to this skill is being able to read *context*. That loud siren in the office might be an emergency; but you've probably learned that it often sounds as a test, and sometimes by mistake. Understanding the context when you hear the siren helps you decide whether to head for the fire exit.

Imagine that we greet each other and you ask: 'How are you?' I say: 'I'm fine.' Now, those words could mean (among other things):

- 'I'm feeling well';
- 'I'm happy';
- 'I was feeling unwell but am now feeling better';
- 'I was feeling unhappy but now feel less unhappy';
- 'I'm not injured; there's no need to help me';
- 'Actually, I feel lousy but I don't want you to know it'; or
- 'Help!'

How do you decide what I mean? By reading the context: the tone of my voice, my posture and the way I look at you (or avoid your gaze); the circumstances in which we meet; your understanding of my wider situation and the past history of our relationship; and so on. In order to decide what I might mean, you have to gather all that contextual information – and more – and add it to the words I've uttered.

And even then, what you understand will still only be a best guess. To increase your understanding, you'd need to ask questions or offer a remark that will draw more information from me. You'd need to continue the conversation.

> There is a paradox in communicating. I cannot expect that you will understand *everything* I tell you; and I cannot expect that you will understand *only* what I tell you.
>
> [with thanks to Patrick Bouvard]

GETTING TO KNOW EACH OTHER

In that simple exchange, how could I help you understand my answer more clearly?

To begin with, I could ask:

'What effect am I having?'

Just as you can guess my meaning by interpreting the context of my answer, I can think about what effect my words, and my behaviour, might be having on you. And I can then adjust my behaviour so that you can understand me more easily. Assuming that I want to continue communicating with you, I might offer more detailed information about my state, or demonstrate by my behaviour that 'fine' means 'comfortable, happy, relaxed and ready to hold a conversation with you'.

And, of course, I'm also now paying attention to you. So I'm now noticing *your* behaviour and *your* words; I'm making a best guess about what they might mean by putting them into context. If you're as effective a communicator as I am, you're now also asking what effect your own behaviour is having on me; and adjusting it in order to increase my understanding.

And so begins a subtle dance between us: a gentle exchange of attention. We start to mirror each other's stance and each other's gestures; our voices begin to chime together, matching rhythm, pace and pitch; we begin to echo each other's words and grammatical structures. We may even begin to anticipate each other's words and finish each other's sentences.

We're establishing rapport.

Rapport is the sense that, below the specific detailed meaning of the words we're using, we understand each other. You may feel that I'm 'on your wavelength'; I may feel that we're 'in tune'. Perhaps we're finding 'common ground'. Deep down, we feel, we're sharing each other's thoughts and feelings.

Building rapport

Most rapport occurs spontaneously. Usually, we don't think about how well we're getting on with someone. But we can also try to build rapport deliberately. And, at that point, rapport becomes more than a desirable behaviour. It becomes a communication skill. (We often call it 'breaking the ice'.)

To develop our rapport-building skills, we need to think about our:

- physical behaviour.

- vocal behaviour; and

- verbal behaviour;

Overwhelmingly, we believe what we see. In the famous sales phrase, 'the eye buys'. If there's a mismatch between what I say and what my body is doing, you're going to believe my body. So building rapport deliberately must begin with giving the *physical* signs of being welcoming, relaxed and open.

The music of the voice is the second key factor. We can vary our *pitch* (how high or low the tone of voice is), *pace* (the speed of speaking) and *volume* (how loudly or softly we speak). If you speak quickly and loudly, and raise the pitch of your voice, you'll sound tense or stressed. And that tension will infect the other person, making them feel uneasy. Create vocal music that is lower in tone, slower and softer, and the other person will relax.

But creating rapport means more than matching body language or vocal tone. We must also match the other person's words, so that they feel we're 'speaking their language'.

Building rapport: a doctor's best practice

Dr Grahame Brown is a medical consultant who wondered why his sessions with patients were so ineffective.

He began to realize that the problem was the way he conducted the interview. Getting the relationship right is, he believes, the key to more effective treatment.

My first priority now is to build rapport with the patient in the short time I have with them.

Instead of keeping the head down over the paperwork till a prospective heartsick patient is seated, then greeting them with a tense smile (as all too many doctors do), I now go out into the waiting room to collect patients whenever possible. This gives me the chance to observe in a natural way how they look, how they stand, how they walk and whether they exhibit any 'pain behaviours', such as sighing or limping.

I shake them warmly by the hand and begin a conversation on our way to the consulting area. 'It's warm today, isn't it? Did you find your way here all right? Transport okay?' By the time we are seated, the patient has already agreed with me several times. This has an important effect on our ensuing relationship – we are already allies, not adversaries...

Next, rather than assuming the patient has come to see me about their pain, I ask them what they have come to see me about. Quite often they find this surprising, because they assume that I know all about them from their notes. But even though I will have read their notes, I now assume nothing. I ask open-ended questions that can give me the most information – the facts which are important to them.

From *Human Givens* by Joe Griffin and Ivan Tyrrell, HG Publishing 2004

For most of us, starting a conversation with someone we don't know is stressful. We can be lost for words. 'Breaking the ice' is a skill many of us would dearly love to develop.

The key is to decrease the tension in the encounter. Look for something in your shared situation to talk about; then ask a question relating to that. The other person must not feel excluded or interrogated, so avoid:

- talking about yourself; and

- asking the other person a direct question about themselves.

Doing either will *increase* the tension in the conversation. As will doing nothing! So take the initiative. Put them at ease, and you will soon relax yourself.

Building rapport: the conversational gambit

Here's a simple method to establish rapport with someone you don't know. Try it out at social gatherings, networking meetings and conferences.

1 Copy the other person's body language to create a 'mirror image'.

2 Ask three questions – but no more than three until you've done the next two things.

3 Find something from what you've just learned that will allow you to compliment the other person – subtly.

4 Find something in what you have found out to agree with.

5 Repeat until the conversation takes on a life of its own.

[With thanks to Chris Dyas]

There's a vitally important point to make about building rapport deliberately.

The other person mustn't notice what you're doing.

Once we become aware that someone is consciously trying to put us at our ease, we may begin to feel manipulated and uneasy; and we may begin to lose trust in them. This unease can arise even in situations, like social gatherings or networking events, where we all know that we're playing the rapport-building game. If it doesn't feel natural to us, we're unlikely to respond positively. Subtlety is essential.

A NEW DEFINITION OF COMMUNICATION

We need a new definition of the word 'communication'. After all this discussion of attention, and pattern-matching, and rapport-building, it's clear that we need to replace the transmission model of communication with something more accurate. And the history of the word itself gives us a clue. 'Communication' derives from the Latin *communis*, meaning 'common', 'shared'. It belongs to the family of words that includes *communion, communism* and *community*. When we communicate, we are trying to match meanings.

Or, to put it another way:

Communication is the process of creating shared understanding.

There are many ways in which we seek to created mutual understanding: many technologies, processes and social conventions. But the most fundamental medium we use to communicate is conversation. So thinking about the way we hold conversations is a very good way to start improving our communication skills.

In brief

- Communication begins, not with transmission, but with reception.
- To receive information, we have to:
  - pay attention;
  - understand it; and
  - put it in context.
- Communication begins when we start paying attention.
- Understanding is a *pattern-matching* process.

Sometimes, we have to fill in the gaps to make the pattern.

- The key to this skill is being able to read *context*.
- By asking: 'What effect am I having?' in any conversation, we can begin to build rapport.
- We can build rapport deliberately, by managing our:
  - physical behaviour;
  - vocal behaviour; and
  - verbal behaviour.
- Communication is the process of creating shared understanding.
- Conversation is the principal tool we use.

HOW CONVERSATIONS WORK

Conversation is our core communication channel. We talk to each other to build relationships and to swap information. We influence each other's thoughts, feelings and actions by holding conversations. We converse to solve problems, to co-operate and find new things to do. Conversation is our way of imagining the future.

It may be, as one telecom company tells us, good to talk; but conversations aren't always easy. We may find it hard to hold meaningful conversations with our partners, our parents or our children. Communities in conflict can find it all but impossible to start a conversation. And conversations at work, too, can be fraught with difficulty.

You want to improve your communication skills? Start with the conversations you hold.

THE THREE BASIC RULES OF GOOD CONVERSATION

Conversations are verbal dances. The word 'conversation' derives from Latin; it means 'to move around with'.

Like any dance, a conversation has rules and standard moves. The rules allow us to move more harmoniously together, without stepping on each other's toes or getting out of step. Most of us are so adept at conversation that we're unaware of these rules. Only when a conversation goes wrong do we wonder how to put it right. If we use these basic rules, we'll hold better conversations.

The dance of conversation is made up of 'turns'. We take turns to speak and to listen. The first golden rule of good conversation is:

One speaker at a time.

One of the most important skills in conversation is knowing when to take your turn. If you start speaking during the other person's turn, they're likely to feel annoyed or insulted; they'd be within their rights to complain that we've interrupted them. Speakers might tolerate occasional interruptions, but if you interrupt continually, you'll soon become known as inconsiderate, impolite and selfish. To avoid this reputational damage, it's essential to cultivate the skill of turn-taking.

To take turns properly, we need to listen. Only by listening can we work out:

- when to take our turn; and
- what to say.

We rarely think about it, but each turn in the conversation is fraught with potential danger.

- For a start, it's vitally important to *come in on cue* when you take your turn. Leave too long a gap, and the other person might start to worry. Research suggests that a gap of only half a second is long enough to attract notice and provoke embarrassment or concern.

- Secondly, you need to *show that you've been listening*. If you don't do so, it'll look as if you haven't been paying attention; that you're not in the least interested in what the other person has been saying; that you are, in fact, a rather rude person.

- And finally, when it's your turn to speak, *whatever you say has to be relevant* to what the other person has just said. If you say something completely unrelated to their last remarks, they'll start to think that you're not just impolite and rude, but possibly crazy.

A lot rides on our ability to listen well. Get it right, and the conversation will go swimmingly. Get it wrong, and your long-term relationship might be in jeopardy.

Good conversation: Rule One

One speaker at a time.

Think about how you can take your speaking turns more effectively.

- Prepare for the moment when the speaker finishes speaking.
- Find something to say that demonstrates you've been listening to what they said.
- Find a remark that links clearly and directly to their last turn.

The Cooperative Principle

When we're listening in a conversation, we usually make a simple assumption. We assume that both of us – speaker and listener – are trying to generate shared understanding. We call this assumption the Cooperative Principle.

Of course, the Cooperative Principle sometimes breaks down. (Think of a conversation where you were talking at cross-purposes). Sometimes we try deliberately to violate it. (Think of a heated argument). But in general, we use the Cooperative Principle because it makes sense to do so. What's the point of paying attention to a conversation if we're not trying to keep the conversation going?

So the second golden rule of good conversation is:

Assume that the speaker wants to say something meaningful to you.

If you follow this rule, you'll be ready to do two things.

- First, you'll happily ignore any mistakes they make.
- Second, you'll fill in the gaps between their words.

Most of us find it easy to do both. We usually ignore any mistakes speakers make: errors of grammar or logic, for example. We might not even notice those mistakes. Instead, we give the speaker the benefit of the doubt and focus on what they're trying to say.

We're also very good at filling in the gaps. Remember the Kanizsa Triangle we looked at in Chapter 1? Just as we fill in the gaps of that image to make the image of the triangle, so we fill in the gaps in conversations to create meaning.

Filling in the gaps might mean completing a speaker's statement or interpreting it in a particular way. For example, if the speaker says something incomplete, we might complete the statement – in our heads, or out loud. They might say something that seems, on the surface, to be ambiguous, ridiculous, illogical, untrue or irrelevant. Using the Cooperative Principle, we usually assume that the speaker *means* something by speaking in this way, and we try to figure out that meaning.

Only if we *can't* work out what the speaker means will we consider other possibilities: perhaps they're deliberately lying or being obstructive; maybe they're drunk, mentally incapacitated or disturbed.

There's a good reason for making these two assumptions. After all, it will soon be our turn to speak. We'll need to work out:

- *when* to speak; and
- *what* to say.

If we're using the Cooperative Principle, we'll want our next turn in the conversation to be as meaningful as possible. So we'll need to judge when the speaker has finished speaking and is ready to listen; and we'll have to find something to say that's more or less relevant to what they've just said. And, to do those things, we need to work out what the speaker means.

Good conversation: Rule Two

Assume that the speaker wants to say something meaningful to you.

Find the gaps in what they're saying and try to fill them in. If you're not sure what the speaker means, you might need to:

- *complete* what they've said;
- *clarify* something you don't quite understand; or
- *convert* a statement in some way (because it's ironic, sarcastic, exaggerated, understated, metaphorical, or expressed in jargon).

Use your next speaking turn in the conversation to check that you've understood what the speaker has said.

The four maxims of effective conversation

The Cooperative Principle is the foundation for four other assumptions we make in our conversations. These assumptions are based on the work of Paul Grice, a philosopher of language, who calls them *conversational maxims*.

When we're listening, we usually assume that the speaker will:

- speak the **truth** (they won't say what they know to be false; they have evidence for what they are saying);
- say something **relevant** to the purpose of the conversation;
- contribute **adequate** information: as much as is needed for us to understand, and no more; and
- speak **clearly** (they'll use words we understand, avoid ambiguous words, speak only the number of words necessary, and put the words in a clear order).

We can remember these maxims by using a simple acronym.

True

Relevant

Adequate

Clear

It's a good acronym. After all, we can use these four maxims to keep our conversations – well, on *TRAC*. So the third golden rule of effective conversation is:

Keep the conversation on TRAC.

A speaker might violate one of the maxims without meaning to. When they do so, we're likely to become confused; we might try to bring it back on *TRAC* by drawing attention to the violation.

Imagine that Alice asks Bob: 'What's the weather forecast today?' Suppose Bob replies: 'I'm going to the shops at two o'clock.' Alice is likely to think that Bob is violating the maxim of *relevance*. Surely he misheard the question...

Suppose now that Bob replies by giving a detailed five-day weather forecast for the entire continent – or that he simply says 'OK'. Alice might now consider that he's violating the maxim of *adequacy*. Is he being serious? What point is he trying to make?

And suppose that he replies using complex meteorological terms. Alice is likely to think he's violating the maxim of *clarity*. (Unless, of course, Alice is herself an experienced meteorologist.)

Flouting the maxims

In any of these instances, Alice might assume that Bob is violating the maxims without meaning to. But she's more likely to think that he's *flouting* a maxim deliberately, to make a point.

The Cooperative Principle, after all, always assumes that a speaker *wants* to offer meaningful information. If Alice thinks that Bob is flouting a maxim and *apparently* saying something untrue, irrelevant, inadequate or unclear, then she will probably assume that there's some *hidden* meaning in his reply that she needs to work out.

In other words, Alice will decide she needs to fill in the gaps.

Suppose now that, in answer to her question, 'What's the weather forecast today?', Bob replies: 'You'd better wrap up warm'. On the surface, he's flouted the maxim of *relevance*. He's assumed that Alice can contribute the relevant information to connect his answer to her question: wrapping up warm must mean that it's cold outside, even though he's not said so.

Most of us are very good at supplying the relevant information when speakers flout the conversational maxims. We can usually work out the hidden meaning behind their remarks. Sometimes, though, we find ourselves baffled. We can't work out why a speaker's remarks are untrue, irrelevant, inadequate or unclear. Perhaps our previous remarks have been unclear? Perhaps they don't understand our language very well? Perhaps they're unwell...

Using the maxims to improve our conversations

The maxims of conversation weren't originally intended to be instructions. Grice saw them as the assumptions we usually make when we're talking to each other. But we can use his maxims as guidelines to improve our conversations.

Good conversation: Rule Three

Keep the conversation on TRAC.

If in doubt, we can check whether what we're saying – or hearing – is:

- *t*rue;
- *r*elevant;
- *a*dequate; or
- *c*lear.

If you feel that the conversation is going wrong, try using one of the maxims to bring it back on *TRAC*.

The principal way to use the maxims as listeners is to ask questions; the principal way to use them as speakers is to make statements that refer to the maxims in some way.

Keeping the conversation on *TRAC*	
Questions for listeners	**Statements for speakers**
Truth	*Truth*
How do you know that?	This is just what I've been told.
What evidence do you have for	I can't tell you it's true.
saying that?	There's solid evidence for this.
	It was in the papers! It must be
Relevance	true!
How does [what you've just	
said] connect to [what you said	*Relevance*
before]?	I don't know if this is relevant,
What's the connection?	but…
Your point being?	There is a connection here: let
	me show you…
Adequacy	Look, the point I'm trying to
Can you tell me more?	make is…
Can you explain [this word]	
in more detail?	*Adequacy*
I'm getting lost. Can you put it	Do I need to fill in any details for
more simply?	you?
	I can't tell you more. I'm sworn
Clarity	to secrecy.
What does [x] mean?	
Do you mean…?	*Clarity*
In other words…?	I'm not quite sure how to say
	this, but…
	Put in simple terms, this
	means…

WHY DO CONVERSATIONS GO WRONG?

Following the three basic rules will improve our conversations immediately. They're 'quick hits': with a little practice, we can all begin to:

- take our turn more effectively;
- focus on the meaning the speaker is trying to convey; and
- check remarks for truth, relevance, adequacy and clarity.

But conversations will still go wrong. And working out *why* they went wrong may be hard. Conversations are so subtle and they happen so fast, and few of us have been trained in the art of effective conversation. How can we develop our skills beyond the three basic rules?

Broadly, conversations fail because of reasons in one of three areas.

- Context
- Relationship
- Behaviour

These are the three dimensions of conversation. By looking at them, we can begin to understand more clearly how conversations work, why they go wrong, and how we can improve them.

PUTTING CONVERSATIONS IN CONTEXT

All conversations have a context. They happen for a reason. Most conversations form part of a larger conversation: they are part of a process or a developing relationship.

Many conversations fail because one or both of us ignore the context. If we don't check *why* the conversation is happening, we may very quickly start to misunderstand each other.

The problem may simply be that the conversation never happens. People often complain that their managers are not there to talk to.

'I never see him'; 'she has no idea what I do'; 'he simply refuses to listen'. Other obvious problems that afflict the context of the conversation include:

- not giving enough time to the conversation;
- holding the conversation at the wrong time;
- conversing in an uncomfortable, busy or noisy place;
- a lack of privacy;
- distractions.

Less obvious than these problems – but just as important – are the assumptions that we bring to our conversations. We've already seen that we usually hold conversations on the basis of fundamental assumptions: the Cooperative Principle, and the four maxims that help to keep our conversations on *TRAC*. But the wider context of a conversation supplies other assumptions that can obscure these fundamental principles. For example, we might assume that:

- we both know what we are talking about;
- we know how the other person views the situation;
- we shouldn't let our feelings show;
- the other person is somehow to blame for the problem;
- we can be brutally honest;
- we need to solve the other person's problem;
- we're right and they're wrong.

If we leave those assumptions unquestioned, misunderstandings and conflict can quickly arise.

These assumptions derive from our mental models. (We encountered mental models in Chapter 1: the road sign, the Kanisza Triangle. We use mental models to make sense of incomplete or ambiguous information.) For example, I might hold a mental model that we're in business to make a profit; that women have an inherently different management style from men; or that character is determined by some set of national characteristics.

All too often, conversations become conflicts between these mental models. This is **adversarial conversation,** and it's one of the most important and deadly reasons why conversations go wrong. (We'll discuss adversarial conversation in Chapter 3.)

Key factors: context

- **Objectives.** Do you both know why you are holding the conversation?

- **Time.** Is this the right time to be holding this conversation? What is the history behind the conversation? Is it part of a larger process?

- **Place.** Are you conversing in a place that is comfortable, quiet, and free from distractions?

- **Assumptions.** Do you both understand the assumptions that you are starting from? Do you need to explore them before going further?

WORKING OUT THE RELATIONSHIP

Our relationship defines the limits and potential of our conversation. We converse differently with complete strangers and with close acquaintances. Conversations are ways of establishing, fixing or changing a relationship.

Relationships are neither fixed nor permanent. They are complex and dynamic. Our relationship operates along a number of dimensions, including:

- status;
- power;

- role;
- liking.

All of these factors define the territory of the conversation.

Status

We can define status as the rank we grant to another person in relation to us. We normally measure it along a simple scale: we see ourselves as higher or lower in status in relation to another person.

Status is always relative and temporary. (That's why we have to work so hard to establish it: we use *status symbols* precisely because our status in relation to others is always uncertain.) We confer status on others. It's evident in the degree of respect, familiarity or reserve we grant them. We derive our own sense of status from the status we give the other person.

And we do all this through conversation.

Conversations can fail because the status relationship limits what we can say to each other.

- If we feel **low in status** relative to the other person, we may agree to everything they say and suppress strongly held ideas of our own.

- If we feel **high in status** relative to them, we may tend to discount what they say, put them down, interrupt or ignore them. Indeed, these behaviours are ways of establishing or altering our status in a relationship.

Often, the best strategy in a conversation is to find ways of *equalizing* status. If we feel that our status is threatening to rise in relation to the other person, we might try to raise their status (these behaviours are sometimes called 'pulling'). If we feel our status to be low, we might use our turn in the conversation to raise our status (behaviours sometimes called 'pushing').

Pushing and pulling: conversational tactics	
To raise your status ('push'): • State facts • Express how you feel • Use 'I' statements • Propose, suggest, advocate, recommend • Use a clear, controlled voice	To raise their status ('pull'): • Ask questions • Enquire about feelings • Encourage • Praise • Probe • Flatter • Use 'you' and 'we' statements • Find common ground • Talk less

Power

Power is the control we can exert over others. If we can influence or control people's behaviour in any way, we have power over them. John French and Bertram Raven, in the late 1950s, identified five kinds of power.

• **reward power:** the ability to grant favours for behaviour;
• **coercive power:** the ability to punish others;
• **legitimate power:** conferred by law or other sets of rules;
• **referent power:** the 'charisma' that causes others to imitate or idolize;
• **expert power:** deriving from specific levels of knowledge or skill.

Any of these forms of power can distort our conversations.

People may seek to exercise different kinds of power at different points in a conversation. If you have little reward power over the other person, for example, you may try to influence them as an expert. If you lack charisma or respect with the other person, you may try to exert authority by appealing to legitimate or to coercive power.

> ### Convening power: an emergent force
>
> People are beginning to talk about a new form of power. *Convening power* is defined by the Foreign and Commonwealth Office as 'the ability to bring the right people together'. It's the power of 'connectors', who are often at the heart of effective networking. For more, look at Chapter 9.

Role

A role is a set of behaviours that people expect of us. A formal role may be explicitly defined in a job description; an informal role is conferred on us as a result of people's experience of our conversations.

Conversations may fail because our roles are unclear, or in conflict. We tend to converse with each other in role. If the other person knows that your formal role is an accountant, for example, they'll tend to converse with you in that role. If they know that your informal role is usually the devil's advocate, or mediator, or licensed fool, they'll adapt their conversation to that role.

Seeing people in terms of roles can often lead us to label them with that role. As a result, our conversations can be limited by our mental models about those roles.

> ### Meredith Belbin's team roles
>
> Thousands of managers have now used Belbin's questionnaire to locate themselves among his categories of:
>
> - Chair/co-ordinator;
> - Shaper/team leader;
> - Plant/innovator or creative thinker;

- Monitor-evaluator/critical thinker;
- Company worker/implementer;
- Team worker/team builder;
- Finisher/detail checker and pusher;
- Resource investigator/researcher outside the team;
- Expert.

The danger is that people may label themselves with a role and start to operate exclusively within it. Our conversations could then be limited by our perceived roles.

'A team is not a bunch of people with job titles, but a congregation of individuals, each of whom has a role that is understood by other members.'

[Meredith Belbin]

Liking

Conversations can fail because we dislike each other. But they can also go wrong because we like each other a lot!

Liking and disliking can be more complicated than the simple terms suggest. We can find people attractive in many different ways; we can take against them in ways we may not be able – or willing – to articulate. Liking can become an emotional entanglement or even a fully-fledged relationship; dislike can turn a conversation into a long-term vendetta.

Territory

These four factors – status, power, role and liking – define the *territory* of a conversation.

A successful conversation seeks out shared territory: the common ground between us. But we guard our own territory carefully. We can feel invaded if the other person broaches a matter that we feel is out of bounds to them. And we might tiptoe around the borders of an issue because we're uncertain whether we'd be welcome on that part of the other person's territory.

As a result, many conversational rules are about asking and giving permission to enter each other's territory. A conversation's success may depend on whether you give or ask clearly for such permission.

Key factors: relationship

- **Status.** Is there a marked difference in status between you? Why is that? How does this difference affect the way you are behaving towards the other person? How do you think it might be affecting their behaviour?

- **Power.** Can you see power being wielded in the conversation? What kind of power? In which direction? How might you both be affecting the power relationship? How do you want to affect it?

- **Role.** What is your role in this conversation? Think about your formal role (your job title, perhaps, or contractual position) and your informal role. How do people see you acting in conversations? Can you feel yourself falling naturally into any particular role in the conversation?

- **Liking.** How is the conversation being affected by your feelings towards each other? Is the liking or disliking getting in the way of a productive outcome?

- **Territory.** Where are the boundaries? Are you finding common ground? Where can you give permission for the other person to enter your territory? Where can you ask permission to enter theirs?

MANAGING BEHAVIOUR

Conversations are never simply exchanges of words. We also use **non-verbal communication:** the music of our voice, our gestures, the way we move our eyes or hold our body, the physical positions we adopt in relation to each other.

Non-verbal behaviour is largely unconscious. Actors (and con artists) can control their non-verbal behaviour consciously, but it takes a lot of training. Most of us learn body language simply by absorbing and imitating the body language of people around us. As a result, our non-verbal communication will sometimes say things to the other person that we don't intend them to know.

> Under pressure our bodies leak. Our true feelings come gushing out in gestures.
>
> [Tracy Cox]

Conversations often go wrong because we misinterpret non-verbal messages. There are four main reasons for this.

- **Non-verbal messages are ambiguous.** No dictionary can accurately define them. Their meaning can vary according to context. Some people close their eyes to concentrate on what you are saying; others do so to try to avoid paying you attention.
- **Non-verbal messages are continuous.** We can stop talking but we can't stop behaving! Language is bound by the structures of grammar: we can tell when an idea has finished and when the speaker is starting a new one. Non-verbal communication isn't structured in the same way.
- **Non-verbal messages are multichannel.** Everything happens at once: eyes, hands, feet, body position. We interpret non-verbal messages holistically, as a whole impression. This makes them strong but unspecific: we may not be able to pin down what the behaviour is suggesting to us.

- **Non-verbal messages are culturally determined.** Research suggests that a few non-verbal messages are universal: everybody seems to smile when they are happy, for example. Most non-verbal behaviours, however, are specific to a culture. A lot of confusion can arise from the misinterpretation of non-verbal messages across a cultural divide.

Effective communicators manage their behaviour. They work hard to align their non-verbal messages with their words. You may feel that trying to manage your behaviour is dishonest: 'play-acting' a part that you don't feel. But we all act a little when we hold conversations. Managing our behaviour simply means trying to act appropriately.

Eyes and body movement are the most important elements to manage. By becoming more conscious of the way you use your eyes and move your limbs, you can reinforce the effect of your words and encourage the other person to contribute more fully to the conversation. If you keep your limbs and hands still, and look steadily at the speaker while they are speaking, you'll immediately improve the quality of the conversation.

Key factors: managing behaviour

- **Look for clusters.** If you are picking up a group of non-verbal messages that seem to indicate a single feeling, you may be able to trust your interpretation more fully.

- **Consider past experience.** We can interpret more accurately the behaviour of people we know. We certainly notice *changes* in their behaviour. We also interpret patterns of behaviour over time more accurately than single instances.

- **Check your perceptions.** Ask questions. You are interpreting observed behaviour, not reading someone's mind. Check out what you observe and make sure that your interpretation is accurate.

THE USES OF CONVERSATION

Conversation is the core channel of communication between human beings. We use conversations to establish and maintain relationships with each other, to share useful information and to inspire each other to act. This subtle dance of speaking and listening is an essential life skill.

All the other modes of communication that we explore in this book are related, in some way, to conversation. In Chapter 4, we look at the skills of enquiry, which build on our powers of listening. And Chapter 5 looks at the complementary skills of persuasion: how we influence each other's thoughts and feelings by speaking.

Chapters 7 and 8 discuss forms of communication that might not immediately seem to be conversational. The rules in a presentation, for example, differ markedly from those of conversation: nobody is taking turns, for a start. But audiences in presentations increasingly want speakers to adopt a conversational tone: we want presenters to talk *with* us, not *at* us. Similarly, writing would seem to be quite unlike conversation: the whole point of writing to someone is that we're trying to communicate *without* conversing. And yet the new technologies – email, texting, instant messaging, Twitter – are part of a wider trend to bring writing closer to the spoken word – a trend that brings new challenges and the need for new skills.

Finally, in Chapter 9, we look at networking. Increasingly, we need to be able to communicate with strangers, quickly, comfortably and productively. Networking is a new kind of conversation, and it holds the key to success in many areas of our lives.

But first, let's look a little more at conversation: this most powerful and fascinating of communication skills. How can we improve the conversations we hold, at home, at work and in social situations? Chapter 3 provides some suggestions.

In brief

- The three basic rules of good conversation:
  - Only one speaker should speak at a time.
  - Assume that the speaker wants to say something meaningful to you.
  - Keep the conversation on TRAC. As a listener and a speaker, check for:
    - truth
    - relevance
    - adequacy
    - clarity

- Use questions when listening, and statements when speaking.

- To improve the **context** of your conversations, check that:
  - the objectives are clear
  - the time and place are right
  - you're both making the same assumptions to start with

- To improve the **relationship** in your conversations, manage:
  - the status relationship between you;
  - the power dynamics in the conversation
  - the roles you are taking in the conversation;
  - your personal feelings about each other; and
  - whether you are comfortably on common ground.

- And to improve the **non-verbal behaviour** in the conversation:
  - look for clusters;
  - consider past experience; and
  - check your perceptions.

3

SEVEN WAYS TO IMPROVE YOUR CONVERSATIONS

We hold conversations in every part of our lives: at home, with our partners, children and friends; in social situations like parties and community meetings; and at work – including meetings, interviews and impromptu huddles at the watercooler. Many of these conversations are relaxed chats; but many have specific objectives. It's these purposeful conversations that we explore in this chapter. How can we hold more productive and effective conversations when we need to?

In this chapter, we look at seven proven strategies.

- Clarify your objective.
- Structure your thinking.
- Manage your time.
- Find common ground.

- Move beyond argument.
- Summarize often.
- Use visuals.

Don't feel that you must apply all seven at once. Take a single strategy and work at it for a few days. (You should have plenty of conversations to practise on!) Once you feel that you've integrated that skill into your conversations, move on to another.

CLARIFY YOUR OBJECTIVE

Work out at the start of your conversation what you want to achieve from it.

Think of a conversation as a journey you're taking with another person or group. It will very quickly start to wander off track if you don't know where you're going. You'll complete the journey effectively only if you know clearly where you're aiming for.

State your objective clearly at the start. Give a headline. If you know what you want to achieve, make it clear up front.

Headlines

Newspapers rely on headlines to get the story's message across quickly. You can do the same in your conversations.

I want to talk to you about...
I've looked at the plan and I've got some suggestions.
I know you're worried about the sales figures. I've got some clues that might help.
I've called this meeting to make a decision about project X.

Of course, you might decide to change your objective in the middle of the conversation – just as you might decide to change direction in the middle of a journey. That's fine, so long as everyone in the conversation knows what's going on. Too specific an objective at the start might limit your success at the end. In a negotiation, for example: what would you be willing to settle for, and what's not negotiable?

Objectives roughly divide into two categories.

- Exploring a problem
- Finding a solution

When you're thinking about your headline, ask: 'problem or solution?' We often assume that any conversation about a problem is aiming to find a solution – particularly if someone else has started the conversation. As a result, we may find ourselves working towards a solution without accurately defining or understanding the problem. It may be that the other person doesn't *want* you to offer a solution, but simply to talk through the problem with them.

In a meeting, the best place to announce the objectives of the conversation is on the agenda. The word means 'things to be done': use your agenda to list what you want to *do* in the meeting, not just what you want to talk about. For example, rather than 'IT infrastructure' – a bald heading with no sense of an objective – write something like 'Review supplier options for IT grid maintenance and choose preferred bidder'. It may be longer, but at least everyone now knows what they should be talking about, and why.

Preparing for an interview

If you're preparing for an interview – as interviewer or interviewee – think carefully about what you want to achieve.

What's my objective?

Setting a clear objective is the only way you will be able to measure the interview's success.

What do I need?

Think about the information you will need before and during the interview. What are the key areas you need to cover? In what order? What questions do you need to ask? You may need a notepad, flipchart or business card – or other items like samples.

When and where?

When is the interview happening? For how long? The quality of the interview will be strongly influenced by its venue. If you know where you'll be holding the interview, think about how to make the venue as conducive to good conversation as possible. Where will you sit? Where's the window? Is it quiet and distraction-free?

STRUCTURE YOUR THINKING

You can improve your conversations enormously by giving them structure. The simplest way to structure a conversation is simply to break it in half.

We can imagine thinking as a process in two stages. **First-stage thinking** explores reality and names it. It translates experience into ideas. **Second-stage thinking** then manipulates those ideas to achieve a result. Put simply, first-stage thinking is thinking about a problem; second-stage thinking is thinking about a solution.

I sometimes think that we're obsessed with solutions. Under pressure of time and the drive for results, we often leap to second-stage thinking without spending enough time in the first stage. In our frantic search for a solution, we sometimes almost ignore the problem. Problems can be frightening. To stay with a problem – to explore it, to try to understand it further, to confront it and live with it for a few moments – is too uncomfortable. We don't like living with unresolved problems. Better to deal with it: sort it out, solve it, get rid of it.

Give the first stage – the problem stage – as much attention and time as you can. Then give it a little more. Resist the temptation to rush into second-stage thinking. And make sure that all participants in the conversation are at the same stage at the same time.

Of course, we need to link first-stage thinking to second-stage thinking. Skilled conversationalists take care to link:

- the past and the present;
- the problem and the solution;
- requests and answers;
- negative ideas and positive ideas;
- opinions about what's true with speculation about the consequences.

WASP: welcome; acquire; supply; part

We can break down the two stages of thinking into four steps. It's a powerful model for all sorts of objective-driven conversations: interviews, or agenda items in a meeting.

Welcome (First-stage thinking) At the start of the conversation, state your objectives, set the scene and establish your relationship. Why are we talking about this matter? Why *us*?

Acquire (First-stage thinking) The second step is information gathering. Concentrate on finding out as much as possible about the matter, from as many angles as you can. Good listening is vital. This part of the conversation should be dominated by questions.

Supply (Second-stage thinking) Now, at the third step, summarize what you've learnt and begin to work out what to do with the information. Begin to think about how to move forward: the options that present themselves. It's important at this stage of the conversation to remind yourselves of the objective that you set yourselves at the start.

Part (Second-stage thinking) Finally, work out what you've agreed. State explicitly the conversation's outcome: the action that will result from it. Agree explicitly what's going to happen. Who will do it? Is there a deadline? Who's going to check on progress?

WASP gives you a simple framework to make sure that the conversation stays on track and results in a practical outcome.

Four types of conversation

We can make the simple four-stage WASP model more sophisticated. In this developed model, we hold four conversations, for:

- relationship
- possibility
- opportunity
- action

These four conversations may form part of a single, larger conversation; they may also take place separately, at different stages of a process or project.

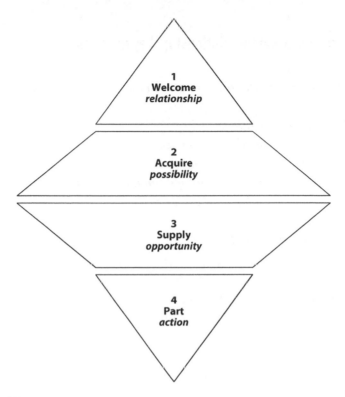

Figure 3.1 Four conversations

A conversation for relationship ('welcome')

This is an exploratory conversation. Hold a conversation for relationship to create or develop the relationship you need to achieve your objective.

A conversation for relationship: key questions

Who are we?
How do we relate to the matter in hand?
What links us?
How do we see things?
What do you see that I can't see?
What do I see that you don't see?
In what ways do we see things similarly, or differently?
How can we understand each other?
Where do we stand?
Can we stand together?

Conversations for relationship are tentative and sometimes awkward or embarrassing. We often rush them. Think of those tricky conversations we hold with strangers at parties. A good conversation for relationship moves beyond the 'What do you do? Where do you live?' questions. We are defining our relationship to each other, and to the matter in hand.

Opening an interview

An effective conversation for relationship is critically important in an interview. Each of you needs to find a way to be at ease, but also to establish the direction of the interview clearly. Beyond the inevitable – and essential – rapport-building questions, the interview needs to be ready with non-invasive questions that invite the interviewee to speak as openly as possible.

Use open questions, that cannot be answered 'yes' or 'no'. Open questions nearly always start with one of the 'w' words: why, who, where, when, what or how.

> *How do you think you've been getting on in the new post?*
> *What would you like to work on in this coaching session?*
> *How can I help you this morning?*
>
> Alternatively, check that the interviewee is clear about why you've arranged the interview.
>
> *I've asked to see you to discuss the possibility of delegating a project to you.*

A conversation for possibility ('acquire')

A conversation for possibility continues the exploration: it develops first-stage thinking. It asks what we *might* be looking at.

A conversation for possibility is *not* about whether to do something, or what to do. It seeks to find new ways of looking at the problem.

There are a number of ways of doing this.

- Look at it from a new angle.
- Ask for different interpretations of what's happening.
- Try to distinguish what you're looking at from what you think about it.
- Ask how other people might see it.
- Break the problem into parts.
- Isolate one part of the problem and look at it in detail.
- Connect the problem into a wider network of ideas.
- Ask what the problem's like. What does it look like, or feel like?

Conversations for possibility are potentially a source of creativity: brainstorming is a good example. But they can also be uncomfortable: exploring different points of view may create conflict. (More about adversarial thinking shortly.)

A conversation for possibility: key questions

What's the problem?
What are we trying to do?
What's the real problem?
What are we really trying to do?
Is this a problem?
How could we look at this from a different angle?
Can we interpret this differently?
How could we do this?
What does it look like from another person's point of view?
What makes this different from last time?
Have we ever done anything like this before?
Can we make this simpler?
Can we look at this in bits?
What is this like?
What does this feel or look like?

Manage this conversation with care. This isn't decision time. If you're chairing a meeting, for example, encourage people to give you ideas, and assure them that you won't hold them to account for them. Take care not to judge or criticize. In an interview, challenge or probe the interviewee's remarks gently. In particular, manage the emotional content of this conversation with care. Ask for the evidence to support expressions of feeling.

The four rules of brainstorming

Groups in meetings are often asked to brainstorm, but meeting leaders don't always understand how brainstorming is supposed to work. Alex Osborn, who invented brainstorming in the late 1930s, offered four rules for an effective brainstorming session.

1 *No criticizing.* Ideas are to be judged later, not during the session.

2 *'Freewheeling' is welcome.* The wilder the idea, the better. It's easier to tame down than to think up.

3 *We want more!* The more ideas, the more the likelihood of a good new one.

4 *Combine and improve.* As well as contributing ideas, team members should suggest ways of improving, combining, or varying others' ideas.

You can develop your brainstorming session in a number of ways to make it even more interesting.

Setting targets

A target of between 50 and 100 ideas in 10 minutes is not unreasonable for a competent team of about 7 people.

Varying the structure

Change the way the session runs by:

- briefing the team with the problem a day beforehand, to allow for private musing and 'sleeping on the problem';
- beginning the session with a warm-up exercise, unrelated to the task in hand;
- taking breaks between techniques, to allow people's minds to relax and discover new ideas.

Separating individual and group brainstorming

An idea is only ever the product of a single mind. Solitary thinking is best for having ideas; group thinking for building on them. Brainstorming can benefit from using both.

A conversation for opportunity ('supply')

A conversation for opportunity takes us into second-stage thinking.

This is fundamentally a conversation about planning. Many of our good ideas never become reality because we don't map out paths of opportunity. A conversation for opportunity constructs such a path. Assess what you would need to make action possible: resources, support and skills. This conversation focuses on future action: in choosing from among a number of possibilities, you're finding a sense of common purpose.

A conversation for opportunity: key questions

Where can we act?
What could we do?
Which possibilities do we build on?
Which possibilities are feasible?
What target do we set ourselves?
Where are the potential obstacles?
How will we know that we've succeeded?

The bridge from possibility to opportunity is *measurement*. Begin to set targets, milestones, obstacles, measures of success. How will you be able to judge when you've achieved an objective?

Recall your original objective. Has it changed? Place yourselves in a future where you've achieved your objective. What does such a future look like and feel like? What's happening? How can you plan more effectively? Usually we plan by starting from where we are and work forwards. By 'backward planning' from an imagined future, we can find sometimes simplify the plan and find new opportunities for action.

A conversation for action ('part')

This is where you agree what to do, who will do it and when it will happen. Translating opportunity into action needs more than agreement; you need to generate a promise, a commitment to act.

A conversation for action is absolutely essential at the end of an interview or meeting. The value of these formal conversations is in the actions that result from them; if nobody's clear who's going to do what, the interview or meeting will have wasted everyone's time.

A conversation for action: key stages

A conversation for action is a dynamic between asking and promising. It takes a specific form.

- You ask the other person to do something by a certain time. Make it clear that this is a request, not an order. Orders may get immediate results, but they rarely generate commitment.

- The other person has four possible answers to this request.
  - They can accept.
  - They can decline.
  - They may commit to accepting or declining at a later date. (*I'll let you know by…*)
  - They can make a counter-offer. (*I can't do that, but I can do…*)

- The conversation results in a promise. *I will do x for you by time y.*

This four-stage model of conversation – either in its simple, WASP form, or in the more sophisticated form of relationship-possibility-opportunity-action – will serve you well. Some of your conversations will include all four stages; some will concentrate on one more than another.

These four conversations will only be truly effective if you hold them *in order*. The success of each conversation depends on the success of the conversation before it. If you fail to resolve a conversation, it will continue underneath the next *in code*. Unresolved aspects of a conversation for relationship, for instance, can become conflicts of possibility, hidden agendas or 'personality clashes'. Possibilities left unexplored become lost opportunities. And promises to act that have no real commitment behind them will create problems later.

Reinforcing commitment

We're more likely to fulfil our promises if we state them publicly or write them down.

- At the end of a meeting, go round the table asking each action-taker to state what they will do, and by when.
- At the end of an interview, both interviewer and interviewee should spend a moment agreeing *and writing down* what each will do.

MANAGE YOUR TIME

Conversations take time, and time is the one entirely non-renewable resource. Manage time well, both for and in your conversations.

Managing time for the conversation

Work out how much time you have. Don't just assume that there is *no* time. Be realistic. If necessary, make an appointment to hold the interview later, or schedule the meeting for another time.

Managing time in the conversation

Most conversations proceed at a varying rate. Generally, an effective conversation will probably start quite slowly and get faster as it goes on. But there are no real rules about this.

You know that a conversation is going too fast when people interrupt each other a lot, when parallel conversations start, when people stop listening to each other and when people start to show signs of becoming uncomfortable.

Reasons why conversations go too fast

- We become solution-oriented
- Feelings take over
- We succumb to 'groupthink' (everybody starts thinking alike to reinforce the group)
- We're enjoying ourselves too much
- Assumptions go unchallenged
- People stop asking questions
- Arguments flare up

Conversely, you know that a conversation is slowing down when one person starts to dominate the conversation, when questions dry up, when people pause a lot, when the energy level in the conversation starts to drop or when people show signs of weariness.

Reasons why conversations go too slowly

- The conversation becomes problem-centred
- Too much analysis is going on
- People talk more about the past than the future
- More and more questions are asked
- People start to repeat themselves
- The conversation wanders
- People hesitate before saying anything

Try to become aware of how fast the conversation is proceeding, and how fast you think it *should* be going. Here are some simple tactics to help you regain control of time in your conversations.

To slow down a conversation	To speed up a conversation
• Reflect what the other person says rather than replying directly to it. • Summarize their remark before moving on to your own. • Go back a stage in the conversation. • Ask open questions: questions that can't be answered 'yes' or 'no'. • Pause. Take a break. • Use the Ladder of Inference. (See below.)	• Push for action. 'What shall we *do*?' 'What do you propose?' • Summarize and close one stage of the conversation. • Look for the implications of what the other person is saying. 'What does that mean in terms of…?' 'How does this affect our plans?' 'So what action is possible here?' • Ask for new ideas and offer some new ones of your own.

Speeding up is probably a more common cause of conversation failure than slowing down. Try to slow the conversation down consciously, and allow time for first-stage thinking. This technique is an integral part of the skills of enquiry, which we explore further in Chapter 4.

FIND COMMON GROUND

Conversations are ways of finding common ground. We mostly begin conversations in our own private territory and use the conversation to find boundaries and the openings where we can cross onto the other person's ground.

We ask for, and give, permission for these moves to happen. If you're asking permission to move into new territory, you might:

- make a remark tentatively;
- express yourself hesitantly: 'perhaps we might...' 'I suppose I think...' 'It's possible that...';
- pause before speaking;
- look away or down a lot;
- explicitly ask permission: 'Do you mind if I mention...' 'May I speak freely about...';
- make a tentative remark about the other person's words or behaviour.

Don't proceed until the other person has given their permission. Such permission may be explicit: 'please say what you like'; 'I would really welcome your honest opinion'; 'I don't mind you talking about that'. Other signs of permission might be in the person's body language or behaviour: nodding, smiling, leaning forward.

Conversely, refusing permission can be explicit – 'I'd rather we didn't talk about this' – or in code. The person may evade your question, wrap up an answer in clouds of mystification or reply with another question. Their non-verbal behaviour is more likely to give you a hint of their real feelings: folding their arms, sitting back in the chair, becoming restless, evading eye contact.

Finding common ground can be especially important in an interview. An interviewee may be intimidated by meeting on the interviewer's territory, for example; and the whole purpose of an interview might be to allow the interviewer more access to the interviewee's private territory. The interview may fail if permission to cross boundaries is not asked for or given.

MOVE BEYOND ARGUMENT

We tend to be better at talking than at listening. At school, we're trained in the techniques of presenting, explaining and arguing for our ideas. We're taught the virtues of *advocacy*: of taking a position, holding it, defending it, convincing others of its worth and attacking any position that threatens it.

As a result, our conversations have a habit of becoming **adversarial**. Instead of searching out the common ground, we hold our own corner and treat every move by the other person as an attack. Adversarial conversations set up a boxing match between competing mental models.

In an attempt to impose some order on this conflict, we've invented debate (from the Latin, 'to beat down'). A debate is a conflict of rigid opinions. By the rules of debate, your opinions are somehow proved to be correct if you can successfully discredit any opposing opinions. You don't even have to prove that an idea is wrong; merely by ridiculing or discrediting the person voicing it, you may be able to influence others to accept your opinion. (Such a move is sometimes called an *ad hominem* argument.)

Opinions are ideas gone cold. They're our assumptions about what should be true, rather than conclusions about what is true in specific circumstances. Our opinions might include:

- stories (about what happened, what may have happened, why it happened);
- explanations (of why something went wrong, why we failed);

- justifications for doing what we did;
- gossip (perhaps to make us feel better at the expense of others);
- generalizations (to save us the bother of thinking);
- wrong-making (to establish power over the other person).

We often mistake opinions for the truth. Whenever you hear someone saying that something is 'a well established fact', you can be certain that they're voicing an opinion.

Adversarial conversation stops the truth from emerging. Arguing actually stops us exploring and discovering ideas. And the quality of the conversation rapidly worsens: people are too busy defending themselves, too frightened, too battle-fatigued, to do any better.

Moving beyond argument in meetings

Adversarial thinking often disrupts meetings. It can emerge in four ways.

Critical thinking

Critical thinking always seeks what's wrong with an idea. Simply to find fault is a very limited way of assessing an idea's value. It can also easily sound like a criticism of the idea holder.

> *To counter critical thinking, ask specifically for positive responses to an idea: 'What's good about it?'*

Ego thinking

'I am my idea.' Once we identify ourselves with ideas, they become opinions. We are so used to opinions that we easily mistake them for the truth.

> *To counter ego thinking, ask for evidence to support opinions. Ask: 'In what circumstances?' Evaluate ideas for their relevance to objectives.*

Political thinking

When ideas become opinions, voicing an idea becomes a political act. To attack an idea is to attack its sponsor; to support it is to create an alliance. We use conversation to create 'power bases' and undermine 'opponents', manipulate ideas, send up smoke screens, foment dissent or spread rumour.

To counter political thinking, invite the whole group to think systematically. Ask for positive and negative responses to an idea in order. Develop this approach by using tools such as SWOT analysis (strengths, weaknesses, opportunities and threats), asking the group to concentrate on one aspect at a time.

Rigid thinking

Adversarial thinking sets ideas against each other. If an idea is to survive the battle, it must become rigid. A debate is a conflict of rigid ideas. Debate is probably the only organized conversation we know. It is also the least effective.

To counter rigid thinking, ask: 'What if?' Look deliberately for the assumptions behind ideas and challenge them. Ask how the matter would look from a radically different perspective. Turn ideas upside down and see what happens.

The Ladder of Inference

The Ladder of Inference takes our conversations beyond argument. The model was developed initially by Chris Argyris. He pictures the way we think in conversations as a ladder. At the bottom of the ladder is observation; at the top, action.

- From our observation, we step onto the first rung of the ladder by selecting **data**. (We choose what to look at.)
- On the second rung, we infer **meaning** from our experience of similar data.
- On the third rung, we generalize those meanings into **assumptions**.
- On the fourth rung, we construct mental models (or **beliefs**) out of those assumptions.
- We act on the basis of our mental models.

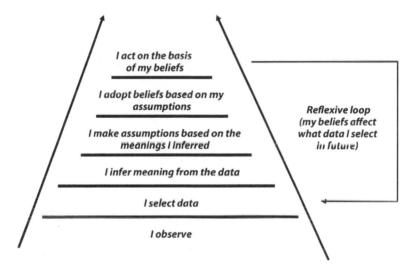

Figure 3.2 The Ladder of Inference

We travel up and down this ladder whenever we hold a conversation. We're often much better at climbing up than stepping down. In fact, we can leap up all the rungs in a few seconds. These 'leaps of abstraction' allow us to act more quickly but they can also limit the course of the conversation. Even more worryingly, our mental models help us to select data from future observation, further limiting the range of the conversation. Argyris calls this a 'reflexive loop'; you might call it a mindset.

The Ladder of Inference gives us more choices about where to go in a conversation. It *slows down* our thinking. It allows us to:

- become more aware of our own thinking;
- make that thinking available to others;
- ask others about their thinking.

Above all, we can defuse an adversarial conversation by 'climbing down' from private beliefs, assumptions and opinions and then 'climbing up' to shared meanings and beliefs.

The key to using the Ladder of Inference is to ask questions. The point is not to use it to score points but to find the differences in the way we think, what we have in common and how we might reach shared understanding.

- *What's the data that underlies what you've said?*
- *Do we agree on the data?*
- *Do we agree on what they mean?*
- *Can you take me through your reasoning?*
- *When you say [what you've said], do you mean [my rewording of it]?*

For example, if one of us suggests a course of action, the other can carefully climb down the ladder by asking:

- *'Why do you think this might work?' 'What makes this a good plan?'*
- *'What assumptions do you think you might be making?' 'Have you considered…?'*
- *'How would this affect…?' 'Does this mean that…?'*
- *'Can you give me an example?' 'What led you to look at this in particular?'*

Even more powerfully, the Ladder of Inference can help us offer our own thinking for the other person to examine. If we are suggesting a plan of action, we can ask them:

- 'Can you see any flaws in my thinking?'
- 'Would you look at this stuff differently?' 'How would you put this together?'
- 'Would this look different in different circumstances?' 'Are my assumptions valid?'
- 'Have I missed anything?'

The beauty of this model is that you need no special training to use it. You can use it immediately, as a practical way to intervene in conversations that are descending into argument.

SUMMARIZE OFTEN

Summarizing is perhaps the most important conversation skill to develop. Summaries help us to do everything else we have been discussing in this chapter.

Why summarize?

- **Summaries allow us to state our objective,** return to it and check that we have achieved it.
- **Summaries help us to structure our thinking,** by recalling where we are in the two stages of thinking, which conversation stage we have reached and where we now need to go.
- **Summaries help us to manage time more effectively** by keeping us from digressing and moving the conversation on when necessary.
- **Summaries help us to seek the common ground between us.** By summarizing what the other person is saying in our own words, we find our own way of inhabiting their territory.
- **Summaries help us to move beyond adversarial thinking.** It's simply harder to disagree with the last remark if you have to summarize it first.

Simple summaries are useful at key turning points in a conversation. At the start, summarize your most important point or your objective. As you move on from one stage to the next, summarize where you think you have both got to, and check that the other person agrees with you. At the end of the conversation, summarize what you have achieved and the action steps you both need to take.

Summarizing isn't merely parroting what the other person has just said. To summarize means to reinterpret their ideas in your own language. It involves:

- **recognizing** the specific point they've made;
- **appreciating** the position from which they say it; and
- **understanding** the beliefs that inform that position.

Recognizing what someone says doesn't imply that you agree with it. It does imply that you have taken the point into account. Appreciating their feelings on the matter doesn't mean you feel the same way, but it does show that you respect those feelings. And understanding the belief may not mean that you share it, but it does mean that you consider it important. All of which means that summaries can contribute to shared problem-solving.

Summarizing in meetings and interviews

Meetings and interviews benefit greatly from regular and scheduled summaries.

A summary from the Chair at the end of an agenda item allows the group to rest, reflect and prepare for the next item. A summary can be even more effective if delivered by a minute-taker from their notes.

An interviewer can use summaries to signal different stages in the interview, to check their understanding of what's been discussed and to allow the interviewee to add or alter information they've offered. A summary is also a good moment to shift the balance of the conversation – the interviewer can invite questions from the interviewee, for example.

USE VISUALS

Apparently, we remember about 20 per cent of what we hear, and over 80 per cent of what we see. Yet most of our conversations don't seem to include a visual element. If communication is the process of displaying our thinking, our conversations will certainly benefit from some way of being able to *see* our ideas.

There are indeed lots of ways in which we can make our thinking visible. The obvious ways include scribbling on the nearest bit of paper or using a flip chart. Less obvious visual aids include the gestures and facial expressions we make. Less obvious still – but possibly the most powerful – are word pictures: the images we can create in each other's minds with the words we use.

Recording your ideas on paper

Conversations nearly always benefit from being recorded visually – especially group conversations like meetings. The patterns and pictures and diagrams and doodles that we scribble on a pad help us to listen, to summarize and to keep track of what we've covered. More creatively, they can become the *focus* for the conversation: in making the shape of our thinking visible on the page, we can ensure that we are indeed covering the same ground together and seeing the relationships between ideas in the same way.

Recording ideas visually – on a pad or a flipchart – also makes conversations more democratic. Once on paper, ideas become common property: all parties to the conversation can see them, add to them, comment on them and combine them.

What we really need, of course, is a technique that's flexible enough to follow the conversation wherever it might go: a technique that can accommodate diverse ideas while maintaining our focus on a clear objective. If the technique could actually help us to develop new ideas, so much the better.

Fortunately, such a technique exists. It's called mind mapping. Mind maps are powerful first-stage thinking tools. By emphasizing the links between ideas, they encourage us to think more creatively and efficiently.

To make a mind map

- Put a visual image of your subject in the centre of a plain piece of paper.

- Write down anything that comes to mind that connects to the central idea.

- Write single words, in BLOCK CAPITALS, along lines radiating from the centre.

- Main ideas will tend to gravitate to the centre of the map; details will radiate towards the edge.

- Every line must connect to at least one other line.

- Use visual display: colour, pattern, highlights.

- Identify the groups of ideas that you have created. If you wish, give each a heading and put the groups into a number order.

Mind maps are versatile conversational tools. They can help us in any situation where we need to record, assemble, organize or generate ideas. They force us to listen attentively, so that we can make meaningful connections; they help us to concentrate on what we are saying, rather than writing; and they store complicated information on one sheet of paper.

Try out mind maps in relatively simple conversations, to begin with. Record a phone conversation using a mind map and see how well you get on with the technique. Extend your practice to face-to-face conversations and invite the other person to look at and contribute to the map. Mind maps can be powerful aids in meetings, when the dynamics of conversation become more complicated. Many managers use them to record the meeting prior to writing minutes.

Instead of drawing mind maps, we could use sticky notes to record ideas. By placing one idea on each note, you can then assemble the notes on a wall or tabletop and move them around to find logical connections or associations between them. Sticky notes are particularly useful in brainstorming sessions or when we are seeking to solve complex problems.

Using metaphors

Metaphors are images of ideas in concrete form. The word means 'transferring' or 'carrying over'. A metaphor carries your meaning from one thing to another. It enables your listener to *see* something in a new way, by picturing it as something else. Metaphor uses the imagination to support and develop your ideas.

Analogies perform much the same function as metaphors. Analogies tell us that one thing is *like* another; metaphors tell us that one thing *is* actually another. If I say that our competitors are forcing us to change our strategy 'like a goalie moving the goalpost', I'm using an analogy. If I say, more simply, 'our competitors are shifting the goalposts', I'm using a metaphor. Metaphor is usually a more powerful way of transforming your idea into an image than analogy.

Metaphors bring your meaning alive in the listener's mind. They narrow our focus and direct our attention to what the speaker wants us to see. They stir our feelings. Metaphor can build our commitment to another person's ideas and help us to remember them.

If you want to find a metaphor to make your thinking more creative and your conversations more interesting, you might start by simply listening out for them in the conversation you are holding. We use many metaphors without even noticing them. If you are still looking, you might try asking some simple questions:

- What's the problem like?
- If this were a different situation – a game of cricket, a medieval castle, a mission to Mars, a kindergarten – how would we deal with it?

- How would a different kind of person manage the issue: a gardener, a politician, an engineer, a hairdresser, an actor?
- What does this situation *feel* like?
- If this problem were an animal, what species of animal would it be?
- Describe what's going on as if it were in the human body.

Explore your answers to these questions and develop the images that spring to mind. You need to be in a calm, receptive frame of mind to do this: the conversation needs to slow down and reflect on its own progress. Finding metaphors is very much part of first-stage thinking, because metaphors are tools to help us see reality in new ways.

You will know when you've hit on a productive metaphor. The conversation will suddenly catch fire (that's a metaphor!). You will feel a sudden injection of energy and excitement as you realize that you are thinking in a completely new way.

In brief

- There are seven proven strategies to help you improve your conversations.
  - Clarify your objective.
  - Structure your thinking.
  - Manage your time.
  - Find common ground.
  - Move beyond argument.
  - Summarize often.
  - Use visuals.
- To clarify your objective:
  - state your objective clearly at the start.
  - ask: problem or solution?

- To structure your thinking:
  - use first-stage thinking and second-stage thinking.
  - use the WASP structure: welcome; acquire; supply; part
  - hold conversations for:
  - relationship
  - possibility
  - opportunity
  - action
- To manage your time:
  - manage time for the conversation
  - manage time in the conversation
- To find common ground:
  - ask for permission to move onto the other person's territory
  - give permission for the other person to move onto your territory
- To move beyond argument:
  - use the Ladder of Inference to check the other person's thinking
  - use the Ladder of Inference to invite the other person to check your thinking
- Summarize:
  - at the start of the conversation
  - regularly throughout the conversation
  - at the end of the conversation
- Use visuals:
  - record your ideas
  - use mindmaps
  - use metaphors

THE SKILLS OF ENQUIRY

The skills of enquiry are the skills of listening. And the quality of your conversation depends on the quality of your listening.

Only by enquiring into the other person's ideas can you respond honestly and fully to them. Only by discovering the mental models and beliefs that underlie those ideas can you explore the landscape of their thinking. Only by finding out how they think can you begin to persuade them to your way of thinking.

Skilled enquiry actually helps the other person to think better. Listening – real, deep, attentive listening – can liberate their thinking.

I've summarized the skills of enquiry under seven headings:

- paying attention;
- treating the speaker as an equal;
- cultivating ease;
- encouraging;
- asking quality questions;

- rationing information;
- giving positive feedback.

Acquiring these skills will help you to give the other person the respect and space they deserve to develop their own ideas – to make their thinking visible.

PAYING ATTENTION

Paying attention means concentrating on what the other person is saying. That sounds simple: how can we listen without paying attention?

Of course, we often do just that. We think we're listening, but we aren't. We finish the other person's sentences. We interrupt. We moan, sigh, grunt, laugh or cough. We fill pauses with our own thoughts, stories or theories. We look at our watch or around the room. We think about the next meeting, or the next report, or the next meal. We frown, tap our fingers, destroy paperclips and glance at our diary. We give advice. We give more advice.

Real listening means shutting down our own thinking and allowing the other person's thinking to enter. If we're paying proper attention, they'll become more intelligent and articulate. Poor attention will make them hesitate, stumble and doubt the soundness of their thinking. Poor attention makes people more stupid.

Listening well means helping the other person to find their ideas. The mind containing the problem probably also contains the solution. Their solution is likely to be much better than ours *because it's theirs*. Paying attention means helping the other person to make their thinking visible.

Of course, the other person may actually want advice. But don't assume that this is the case. Wait for them to ask; if necessary, ask them what they want from you. Don't rush. Give them the chance to find their own ideas first. Paying attention in this way will probably slow the conversation down more than you feel is comfortable. Adjust your own tempo to that of the other person. Wait longer than you want to.

Listen. Listen. And then listen some more. And when they can't think of anything else to say, ask: 'What else do you think about this? What else can you think of? What else comes to mind?' That invitation to talk more can bring even the weariest brain back to life.

Interrupting

Interrupting is the most obvious symptom of poor attention. It's irresistible. Some demon inside us seems to compel us to fill the other person's pauses with words. It's as if the very idea of silence is terrifying.

Mostly, we interrupt because we're making assumptions. Here are a few. Next time you interrupt someone in a conversation, ask yourself which of them you're applying.

- My idea is better than theirs.
- The answer is more important than the problem.
- I have to utter my idea fast and if I don't interrupt, I'll lose my chance (or forget it).
- I know what they're going to say.
- They don't need to finish the sentence because my rewrite is an improvement.
- They can't improve this idea any further, so I might as well improve it for them.
- I'm more important than they are.
- It's more important for me to be seen to have a good idea than for me to let them finish.
- Interrupting will save time.

You're usually wrong when you assume that you know what the other person is about to say. If you allow them to continue, they'll often come up with something more interesting, more vivid and more personal.

Allowing quiet

Once you stop interrupting, the conversation will become quieter. Pauses will appear. The other person will stop talking and you won't fill the silence.

These pauses are like junctions. The conversation has come to a crossroads. You have a number of choices about where you might go next. Either of you might make that choice. If you're interested in persuading, you'll seize the opportunity and make the choice yourself. But, if you're enquiring, then you give the speaker the privilege of making the choice.

There are two kinds of pause. One is a filled pause; the other is empty. Learn to distinguish between the two.

Some pauses are filled with thought. Sometimes, the speaker will stop. They'll go quiet, perhaps suddenly. They'll look elsewhere, probably into a longer distance. They're busy on an excursion. You're not invited. But they'll want you to be there at the cross-roads when they come back. You're privileged that they've trusted you to wait. So wait.

The other kind of pause is an empty one. Nothing much is happening. The speaker doesn't stop suddenly; instead, they seem to fade away. You're standing at the crossroads in the conversation together, and neither of you is moving. The energy seems to drop out of the conversation. The speaker's eyes don't focus anywhere. If they're comfortable in your company, they may focus on you as a cue for you to choose what move to make.

Wait out the pause. If the pause is empty, the speaker will probably say so in a few moments. 'I can't think of anything else.' 'That's it, really.' 'So. There we are. I'm stuck now.' Try asking: 'Can you think of anything else?' Resist the temptation to move the conversation on by asking a more specific question. The moment you do that, you've closed down every other possible journey that you might take together: you're dictating the road to travel. Make sure that you only do so once the other person is ready to let you take the lead.

Showing that you're paying attention

Your face will show the other person whether you're paying attention to them. In particular, your eyes will speak volumes about the quality of your listening.

By behaving *as if* you are interested, you can sometimes *become* more interested.

How to show that you're paying attention

Pay attention! If you actually pay attention, you will look as if you are paying attention.

Relax your facial muscles. Try not to frown. No rigid smiles.

Keep your eyes on the person doing the talking. If you take your eyes away from them, be ready to bring your gaze back to them soon. (The speaker will probably look away frequently: that's what we do when we're thinking.)

Think about the angle at which you are sitting or standing. Sixty degrees gives the speaker's eyes a useful escape lane.

Use minimal encouragers. (For more, look below under 'Encouraging'.)

Make notes. If necessary, ask them to pause while you make your note.

It may be that such attentive looking actually inhibits the speaker. In some cultures, looking equates to staring and is a sign of disrespect. You need to be sensitive to these possible individual or cultural distinctions and adapt your eye movements accordingly. Generally, people do not look nearly enough at those they are listening to. The person speaking will pick up the quality of your attention through your eyes – possibly unconsciously – and the quality of their thinking will improve as a result.

TREATING THE SPEAKER AS AN EQUAL

You will only be able to enquire well if you treat the speaker as an equal. The moment you make your relationship unequal, confusion will result. If you place yourself higher than them in status, you will discourage them from thinking well. If you place them higher than you, you will start to allow your own inhibitions to disrupt your attention to what they are saying.

Patronizing the speaker is the greatest enemy of equality in conversations. This conversational sin derives from the way people are treated as children – and the way some people subsequently treat children. Sometimes children have to be treated like children. It is necessary to:

- decide for them;
- direct them;
- tell them what to do;
- assume that adults know better than they do;
- worry about them;
- take care of them;
- control them;
- think for them.

There is a tendency to carry this patronizing behaviour over into conversations with other adults. As soon as you think you know better than the other person, or provide the answers for them, or suggest that their thinking is inadequate, you're patronizing them. You can't patronize somebody and pay them close attention at the same time.

Treat the other person as an equal and you won't be able to patronize them. If you don't value somebody's ideas, don't hold conversations with them. But if you want ideas that are better than your own, if you want better outcomes and improved working relationships, work hard on giving other people the respect that they and their ideas deserve.

CULTIVATING EASE

Good thinking happens in a relaxed environment. Cultivating ease will allow you to enquire more deeply, and discover more ideas.

Most people aren't used to ease and may actually argue against it. They're so used to urgency that they can't imagine working in any other way. Many organizations dispel ease from the workplace. Ease is equated with sloth. If you're not working flat out, chasing deadlines and juggling 50 assignments at the same time, you're not worth your salary. It's assumed that the best thinking happens in such a climate.

It's a false assumption. Urgency keeps people from thinking well; they're too busy doing. After all, doing is what gets results, isn't it? Not when people have to think to get them. Sometimes, the best results only appear by not doing: by paying attention to someone else's ideas with a mind that's alert, comfortable, and at ease. When you're at ease, the solution to a problem will sometimes appear as if by magic.

How to cultivate ease

Find the time. If the situation is urgent, postpone the conversation.

Make space. A quiet space; a neutral space; a comfortable space.

Banish distractions. Unplug the phones. Leave the building. Barricade the door.

Cultivating ease in a conversation is largely a behavioural skill. Make yourself comfortable. Lean back, breathe out, smile, look keen and slow down your speaking rhythm.

ENCOURAGING

In order to liberate the other person's ideas, you may need to do more than pay attention, treat them as an equal and cultivate ease. You may need to actively encourage them to give you their ideas.

Remember that the other person's thinking is to a large extent the result of the effect you have on them. So if you:

- suggest that they change the subject;
- try to convince them of your point of view before listening to their point of view;
- reply tit-for-tat to their remarks; or
- encourage them to compete with you;

– you aren't encouraging them to develop their thinking. You're not enquiring properly.

Competitiveness is one of the worst enemies of encouragement. It's easy to slip into a ritual of using the speaker's ideas to promote your own. It's all part of the tradition of adversarial thinking that is so highly valued in Western society.

Competition forces people to think only those thoughts that will help them win. If the speaker feels that you are competing with them in the conversation, they will limit not only what they say but also what they think. Similarly, if you feel that the speaker is trying to compete with you, don't allow yourself to enter the competition. This is much harder to achieve. The Ladder of Inference (see Chapter 3) is one very powerful tool that will help you to defuse competitiveness in your conversations.

Instead of competing, welcome the difference in your points of view. Encourage a positive acknowledgement that you see things differently, and that you must deal with that difference if the conversation is to move forward.

Minimal encouragers

Minimal encouragers are brief, supportive statements and actions that convey attention and understanding.

They can be:

- sub-vocalizations: 'uh-huh', 'mm';
- words and phrases: 'right', 'really?', 'I see';
- repeating key words.

Behaviours can include:

- leaning forward;
- focusing eye contact;
- head-nodding.

Benefits of encouragers:

- can support the speaker without interrupting them;
- demonstrate your interest;
- encourage the speaker to continue;
- show appreciation of particular points – successes, ideas the speaker finds important;
- indicate recognition of emotion or deep feeling.

Potential problems of encouragers:

- can be used to direct the course of the conversation – a subtle form of influence;
- can reinforce the speaker's behaviour in a particular direction – they may start to say things in the hope of receiving the 'prize' of a minimal encourager;
- if unsynchronized with other behaviours, may indicate impatience or a desire to move on;
- can become a ritualized habit, empty of meaning.

ASKING QUALITY QUESTIONS

Questions are the most obvious way to enquire into other people's thinking. Questions, of course, can be loaded with assumptions. They can be politically charged. In some conversations, the most important questions are never asked because to do so would be to challenge the centre of authority. To ask a question can sometimes seem like revealing an unacceptable ignorance. In some organizations, to ask them is simply 'not done'. 'Questioning', said Samuel Johnson on one occasion, 'is not the mode of conversation among gentlemen.'

Questions can also be used in ways that don't promote enquiry. Specifically, we sometimes use questions to:

- emphasize the difference between our ideas and other people's;
- ridicule or make the other person look foolish;
- criticize in disguise;
- find fault;
- make ourselves look clever;
- express a point of view in code;
- force the other person into a corner;
- create an argument.

The only legitimate use of a question is to foster enquiry. Questions help you to:

- find out facts;
- check your understanding;
- help the other person to improve their understanding;
- invite the other person to examine your own thinking;
- request action.

The best questions open up the other person's thinking. A question that helps the other person think further, develop an idea or make their thoughts more visible to you both, is a high-quality question.

A whole repertoire of questions is available to help you enquire more fully. Specifically, we can use six types of questions:

- *Closed questions.* Can only be answered 'yes' or 'no'.
- *Leading questions.* Put the answer into the other person's mouth.
- *Controlling questions.* Help you to take the lead in the conversation.
- *Probing questions.* Build on an earlier question, or dig deeper.
- *Open questions.* Cannot be answered 'yes' or 'no'.
- *Reflecting questions.* Restate the last remark with no new request.

Remember also the Ladder of Inference from Chapter 3. This powerful tool can provide questions that allow you to enquire into the speaker's thinking. You can also use it to invite them to enquire into yours.

The highest-quality questions actually liberate the other person's thinking. They remove the assumptions that block thinking and replace them with other assumptions that set it free. The key is identifying the assumption that might be limiting the other person's thinking. You don't have to guess aright: asking the question may tell you whether you've identified it correctly; if it doesn't, it may well open up the speaker's thinking anyway.

These high-quality questions are broadly 'What if' questions. You can either ask a question in the form 'What if this assumption weren't true?' or in the form 'What if the opposite assumption were true?'

Examples of the first kind of question might include:

- What if you became chief executive tomorrow?
- What if I weren't your manager?
- What if you weren't limited in your use of equipment?

Examples of the second kind might include:

- What if you weren't limited by a budget?
- What if customers were actually flocking to us?
- What if you knew that you were vital to the company's success?

People are often inhibited from developing their thinking by two deep assumptions. One is that they are incapable of thinking well about something, or achieving something. The other is that they don't deserve to think well or achieve. Asking good questions can help you to encourage the other person to overcome these inhibitors and grow as a competent thinker.

RATIONING INFORMATION

Information is power. Sometimes, as part of enquiry, you can supply information that will empower the speaker to think better. Withholding information is an abuse of your power over them.

The difficulty is that giving information disrupts the dynamic of listening and enquiring. A few simple guidelines will help you to ration the information that you supply.

- *Don't interrupt.* Let the speaker finish before giving any new information. Don't force information into the middle of their sentence.
- *Time your intervention.* Ask yourself when the most appropriate time might be to offer the information.
- *Filter the information.* Only offer information that you think will improve the speaker's thinking. Resist the temptation to amplify some piece of information that is not central to the direction of their thinking.
- *Don't give information to show off.* You may be tempted to give information to demonstrate how expert or up to date you are. Resist that temptation.

Asking the speaker for information is also something you should ration carefully. You need to make that request at the right time, and for the right reason. To ask for it at the wrong time may close down their thinking and deny you a whole area of valuable ideas.

Following this advice may mean that you have to listen without fully understanding what the speaker is saying. You may even completely misunderstand for a while. Remember that enquiry is about helping the other person clarify their own thinking. If asking for information will help only you – and not the speaker – you should consider delaying your request. In enquiry, it's more important to let the speaker do their thinking than to understand fully what they are saying. This may seem strange, but if you let the speaker work out their thinking rather than keeping you fully informed, they will probably be better able to summarize their ideas clearly to you when they've finished.

GIVING POSITIVE FEEDBACK

Feedback is the way we check that our enquiry has been successful. But feedback can do more. It can prepare us to switch the mode of conversation from enquiry to persuasion. It can also help us to end a conversation; summarizing your response to what the speaker has said and providing the foundations for a conversation for action.

There are two kinds of feedback: positive and negative. It's obvious in simple terms how they differ. Positive feedback is saying that we like, appreciate and value the speaker's ideas. Negative feedback is saying that we dislike them, are hostile to them or place no value on them.

Clearly the two kinds of feedback have wider consequences. Positive feedback encourages the other person to go on thinking. Negative feedback is likely to stop them thinking. Positive feedback also encourages the speaker to value their own thinking; negative feedback tells them that their thinking is worthless. Positive feedback makes people more intelligent. Negative feedback makes them more stupid.

Negative feedback is usually a sign that we are adopting what one consultant calls 'Negative reality norm theory'. This is the theory that only negative attitudes are realistic. We see this theory at work every day in our newspapers. News, almost by definition, is bad news. The phrase 'good news' is virtually a contradiction in terms.

We live out the theory in our everyday lives and in our conversations. To be positive is to be naive and simplistic; it makes us vulnerable. To be negative is to be well informed and protected from the 'slings and arrows of outrageous fortune'. Whenever we say 'we must be realistic', we usually mean that we should emphasize the negative aspects of the situation.

Given this social norm, to be positive can seem like challenging reality. Actually, of course, the positive is merely another part of our picture of reality. In adding it to the negative, we are completing the picture, not distorting it.

The best kind of feedback is *genuine*, *succinct* and *specific*. If you fake it, the other person will rumble you. If you go on, they'll suspect your honesty. If you are too general, they'll find it hard to use the feedback.

Balancing appreciation and criticism

We tend to think of feedback as a one-off activity. Actually, we're feeding back to the speaker all the time we're listening to them. Be sure that the continuous feedback you give indicates your respect for them, as people and as thinkers, even if you disagree with their ideas.

Make sure that your positive feedback outweighs the negative. A good working ratio might be five-to-one: five positive remarks for every negative one. This can sometimes be difficult to achieve! The speaker may not have delivered any very good ideas. It's more likely that you can see only what's bad, or wrong, or incomplete, or inaccurate, about their ideas. Years of training and experience in critical thinking may have taught you not to comment on what you approve or like.

Look for things to be positive about. Get into the habit of asking: 'What's good about what this person is saying?' Force yourself, if necessary, to find some answers to that question; then be sure to give those answers to the speaker. It's easier to ask this question if you adopt a policy of *assuming constructive intent*. You might be assuming that the speaker isn't trying to do their best thinking, or seeking a genuine solution. In fact, they're likely to be trying to think as well as they can. Assume that they're trying to be positive, and give appropriate feedback. One result, among others, is that the speaker will be encouraged to be more constructive.

The more formal the conversation, the more likely that your feedback will be a single, lengthy contribution. You need to choose carefully when to give your feedback. Too early, and you may close the conversation down prematurely. Too late, and the effect may be lost. If in doubt, you can ask whether it's appropriate to start your feedback or whether the speaker wants to continue. Ask:

- for permission to feed back;
- how the speaker sees the situation in summary;
- what the speaker sees as the key issue or problem.

Only then should you launch into your own feedback.

Give your positive feedback before any negative feedback. Make your own objective clear and explain how your feedback relates to that objective. Feedback will naturally become more positive if you make it forward-looking: what you and the other person are trying to achieve, what you both want to do. The best negative feedback is about whatever is hindering progress towards the objective. You can productively ignore any other ideas that you happen to disagree with.

Feed back on ideas and information, rather than on the person. Support any comments you make with evidence. Focus on the key idea or aspect that you think would change the situation most strongly for the better. If you praise them, the speaker is more likely to accept the need to change their views or their behaviour.

In brief

- There are seven key skills of enquiry.

    - Paying attention
    - Treating the speaker as an equal
    - Cultivating ease
    - Encouraging
    - Asking quality questions
    - Rationing information
    - Giving positive feedback

- To pay attention:

    - listen
    - don't interrupt
    - allow quiet
    - show that you're paying attention

- To treat the speaker as an equal:

    - give equal turns to speak and listen
    - don't tell them what to say
    - don't assume that you know what they mean better than they do

- To cultivate ease:

    - find time
    - make space
    - banish distractions

- To encourage:
  - don't compete in the conversation
  - explore differences of opinion
  - use minimal encouragers
- Ask quality questions to help you:
  - find out facts
  - check your understanding
  - help the other person to improve their understanding;
  - invite the other person to examine your own thinking;
  - request action.
- To ration information:
  - don't interrupt
  - time your intervention
  - filter the information
  - don't give information to show off
- To give positive feedback:
  - balance appreciation and criticism
  - assume constructive intent
  - feed back on specifics

THE SKILLS OF PERSUASION

The ability to persuade and influence has never been in more demand. These days we all have to be able to sell our ideas.

Ideas are the currency of persuasion. Information alone will never move anyone to act. Only ideas have the power to influence.

The old word for this power is rhetoric. Since ancient times, the art of rhetoric has taught people how to assemble and deliver their ideas. Few people – at least in Europe – now study rhetoric systematically. Yet, by applying a few simple rhetorical principles, you can radically improve your skills in persuading others.

CHARACTER, LOGIC AND PASSION

Aristotle, the grandfather of rhetoric, claimed that we can persuade in two ways: through the evidence that we can bring to support our case, and through what he called 'artistic' persuasion.

Evidence is whatever we can display to support our case. We might use documents or witnesses; these days, we might use the results of research or focus groups.

'Artistic' persuasion consists of three appeals using the skills of the persuader themselves:

- appealing to the audience through your reputation with them;
- appealing to their reason; and
- appealing to their emotions.

Aristotle's names for these appeals – *ethos*, *logos* and *pathos* – have become well known.

Character (*ethos*)

Rhetoricians realized very early on that people were swayed as much by passions and prejudices as by reason. For example, we tend to believe people whom we trust or respect. *Ethos* is the appeal to our audience through personality, reputation or personal credibility. Why should your listener believe what you are telling them? What are your qualifications for saying all this? How does your reputation stand with them? What value can you add to the argument from your own experience? Your character creates the trust upon which you can build your argument.

Logic (*logos*)

Logic is the work of rational thought. By using *logos*, we're appealing to our audience's ability to reason. We construct an argument, creating reasons to support the case we are making and demonstrating that those reasons logically support the case. Logic comes in two forms: deductive and inductive. (More about logic later in this chapter.)

Passion (*pathos*)

In the end, we're probably influenced to act more by our emotions than by anything else. Appealing to the feelings – *pathos* – is thus a vital element in any attempt to persuade.

Unlike *ethos* and *logos*, the appeal to the audience's emotions will only succeed if it's indirect. We can lay out our argument or our credentials openly, but we cannot *announce* to our audience that we are about to appeal to their emotions; they'll immediately be put on their guard. Neither can we inspire an emotion by talking about it; we must present something external that will arouse emotion. A charitable appeal, for example, might seek to arouse people to donate by showing pictures of children dying in hospital, or animals in distress. Feeling the emotion – or displaying it – may be helpful, but a dispassionate presentation or description will often be more emotionally arousing than an emotional one.

Because it's often indirect, *pathos* often has the reputation of being manipulative, dishonest or unethical. And we know that speakers can inspire audiences to wildly irrational and dangerous behaviour by playing on their emotions. But the abuse of *pathos* doesn't mean we should avoid it. Persuading without emotion is unlikely to be effective, partly because it will seem inhuman (Mr Spock on *Star Trek* continually had this problem when trying to persuade his colleagues to act rationally).

The aim of *pathos* must be to arouse the emotional response that's appropriate to the case arguing. Emotion need not be overwhelming. If we allow the subject matter or the occasion to elicit emotion in the audience, we shall probably exercise *pathos* well.

All three of these qualities – character, reasoning and passion – must be present if you want to persuade someone. The *process* of working out how to persuade them consists of five key elements:

- identifying the core idea;

- arranging your ideas logically;

- developing an appropriate style in the language you use;

- remembering your ideas;

- delivering your ideas with words, visual cues and non-verbal behaviour.

WHAT'S THE BIG IDEA?

If you want to persuade someone, you must have a message. What do you want to say? What's the big idea? A single governing idea is more likely to persuade your listener than a group of ideas, simply because one strong idea is easier to remember.

Begin by gathering ideas. Conduct imaginary conversations in your head and note down the kind of things you might say. Capture ideas as they occur to you and store them on a pad or in a file. Spend as much time as you can gathering material before the conversation itself.

Having captured and stored some ideas, ask three fundamental questions:

- *'What is my objective?'* What do I want to achieve? What would I like to see happen?

- *'Who am I talking to?'* Why am I talking to this person about this objective? What do they already know? What more do they need to know? What do I want them to do? What kind of ideas will be most likely to convince them?

- *'What is the most important thing I have to say to them?'* If I were only allowed a few minutes with them, what would I say to convince them – or, at least, to persuade them to keep listening?

Think hard about these three questions. Imagine that you had only a few *seconds* to get your message across. What would you say?

Try to create a single sentence. You can't express an idea without uttering a sentence. Above all, this idea should be *new* to the listener. After all, there's no point in trying to persuade them of something they already know or agree with!

Once you've decided on your message, consider whether you think that it's appropriate, both to your objective and to your listener. Does this sentence express what you want to say? Is it in language that the listener will understand easily? Is it simple enough?

Now test your message sentence. If you were to speak this sentence to your listener, would they ask you a question? If so, what would that question be? If your message is a clear one, it will provoke *one* of these three questions:

- 'Why?'
- 'How?'
- 'Which ones?'

If you can't imagine your listener asking any of these questions, they're unlikely to be interested in your message. So try another. If you can imagine them asking more than one of these questions, try to simplify your message.

Now work out how to bring your listener to the place where they will accept this message. You must 'bring them around to your way of thinking'. This means starting where the listener is standing and gently guiding them to where you want them to be. Once you are standing in the same place, there's a much stronger chance that you'll both see things the same way. Persuading them will become a great deal easier.

People will only be persuaded by ideas that interest them. Your listener will only be interested in your message because it answers some need or question that already exists in their mind. An essential element in delivering your message, then, is demonstrating that it relates to that need or that question.

Here is a simple four-point structure that will bring your listener to the point where they can accept your message. I remember it by using the letters SPQR (which is the motto of the Roman Empire).

Situation

Briefly tell the listener something they already know. Say something about the matter that you *know* they'll agree with. You're showing that you're on their territory: you understand their situation and can appreciate their point of view. Try to state the Situation so that the listener expects to hear more. Think of this as a kind of 'Once upon a time...'. It's an opener, a scene-setting statement that prepares them for what's to come.

Problem

Now identify a Problem that has arisen within the Situation. The listener may know about the Problem; they may not. But they certainly *should* know about it! In other words, the Problem should be *their* problem.

What's the problem?

Situation	Problem
Stable, agreed status quo	Something's gone wrong
	Something could go wrong
	Something's changed
	Something could change
	Something new has arisen
	Someone has a different point of view
	We don't know what to do
	There are a number of things we could do

Problems, of course, come in many shapes and sizes. It's important that you identify a Problem that the listener will recognize. It must clearly relate to the Situation that you're set up: it poses a threat to that Situation, or creates a challenge within it.

Problems can be positive as well as negative. You may want to alert your listener to an opportunity that has arisen within the Situation.

Question

The Problem causes the listener to ask a Question (or would do so, if they were aware of it). Once again, the listener may or may not be asking the Question. If they are, you're better placed to answer it. If they're not, you may have to carefully persuade them to agree that this Question is worth asking.

What's the question?

Situation	Problem	Question
Stable,	Something's gone wrong	What do we do?
agreed	Something could go	How do we stop it?
status quo	wrong	
	Something's changed	How do we adjust to it?
	Something could change	How do we prepare for it?
	Something new has arisen	What can we do?
	Someone has a different point of view	Who's right?
	We don't know what to do	What do we do? or How do we choose?
	There are a number of things we we could do	Which course do we take?

Response

Your Response or answer to the Question should be your message. In other words, the Message should naturally emerge as the answer to the Question raised in the listener's mind by the Problem!

SPQR is a classic story-telling framework. It's also well known as a method management consultants use in the introductions to their proposals. The trick is to take your listener through the four stages *quickly*. Don't be tempted to fill out the story with lots of detail. As you use SPQR, remember these three key points:

1 SPQR should *remind* the listener rather than persuade them. Until you get to the message, you shouldn't include any idea that you would need to prove.

2 Think of SPQR as a story. Keep it moving. Keep the listener's interest.

3 Adapt the stages of the story to the needs of the listener. Make sure that they agree to the first three stages without difficulty. Make sure that you are addressing their needs, values and priorities. Put everything in their terms.

ARRANGING YOUR IDEAS

Logic is the method by which you assemble ideas into a coherent structure. So you must have a number of key ideas that support the message you have chosen. Ideally, they are answers to the question you can imagine your listener asking when you utter your message.

Finding your key ideas

If your message provokes the listener to ask:	*Your key ideas will be:*
'Why?'	Reasons, benefits or causes
'How?'	Methods, ways to do something, procedures
'Which ones?'	These ones: items in a list

There are two ways to organize ideas logically. They can be organized deductively, in a sequence, and inductively, in a pyramid.

Arguing deductively

Deductive logic takes the form of a syllogism: an argument in which a conclusion is inferred from two statements (see Figure 5.1). To argue deductively:

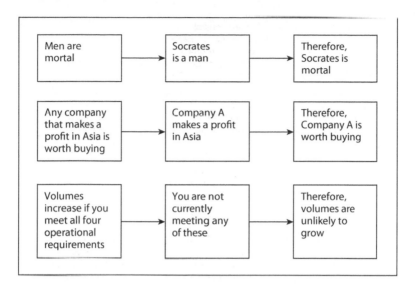

Figure 5.1 Some examples of deductive reasoning

- make a statement;
- make a second statement that relates to the first – by commenting on either the subject of the first statement, or on what you have said about that subject;
- state the implication of these two statements being true simultaneously. This conclusion is your message.

Arguing inductively

Inductive logic works by stating a governing idea and then delivering a group of other ideas that the governing idea summarizes. Another name for this kind of logic is *grouping and summarizing*.

Inductive logic creates pyramids of ideas (see Figure 5.2). You can test the logic of the structure by asking whether the ideas in any one group are answers to the question that the summarizing idea provokes. (You've done this already when formulating your message.) That question will be one of three: 'Why?', 'How?' or 'Which ones?'

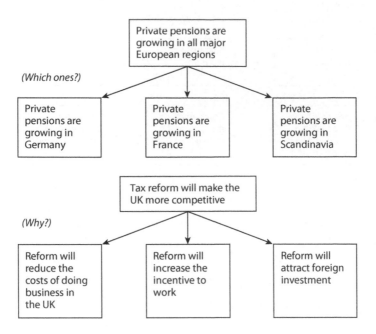

Figure 5.2 Some examples of inductive reasoning

Inductive logic tends to be more powerful in business than deductive logic. Deductive logic brings two major risks with it.

1 It demands real patience on the part of the listener. If you put too many ideas into your sequence, you may stretch their patience to breaking point.

2 You may undermine your own argument. Each stage in the deductive sequence is an invitation to the listener to disagree. And they only have to disagree with one of the stages for the whole sequence to collapse.

Inductive logic avoids both of these perils. First, it doesn't strain the listener's patience, because the main idea – the message – appears at the beginning. Second, a pyramid is less likely to collapse than a strung-out sequence of ideas: you can see more clearly whether your other ideas support your message. And the message has a good chance of surviving even if one of the supporting ideas is removed. Pyramids of ideas satisfy our thirst for answers now and evidence later. They allow you to be more creative in assembling your ideas and they put the message right at the front.

Deductive logic is only really useful for establishing whether something is true. Inductive logic can also help you to establish whether something is *worth doing*.

EXPRESSING YOUR IDEAS

It's not enough to have coherent ideas, logically organized. You have to bring the ideas alive in the listener's mind. You have to use words to create pictures and feelings that will stimulate their senses as well as their brain.

We don't remember words. We forget most of what others tell us. But we *do* remember images – particularly images that excite sensory impressions and feelings. If you can stimulate your listener's imagination through the senses and arouse some feeling in them, you will be able to plant the accompanying idea in their long-term memory.

Memory = image + feeling

The word 'image', of course, powerfully suggests something visual. But you can create *impressions* through any of the five senses: sight, hearing, touch, smell and taste. Some people will be convinced by pictures; others will only be persuaded if they hear the words come out of their own mouth. Others again will only remember and learn by touching: they are the 'hands-on' people who demand demonstrations and practice.

Neuro-linguistic programming (NLP) works on the basis of people's natural sensory preferences for receiving information. NLP seeks to develop this awareness of sensory preference into a systematic approach to communicating.

Even without training or study, however, you can become more attuned to the way you respond to ideas with your senses.

Whenever you are seeking to persuade someone with an idea, think about how each of the five senses might respond to it. Try to create an impression of the idea that will appeal to one or other of the senses. You'll find that the idea comes magically alive.

Examples

Perhaps the simplest way to bring an idea alive is to offer a concrete example. Find an instance where the idea has been put into practice, or where it has created real results – either useful or disastrous.

Examples can be powerfully and immediately persuasive. Concrete instances and applications of ideas make us take the ideas more seriously.

Stories

Stories are special kinds of examples. They lend weight to the example by bringing it alive. They also have the benefit of entertaining the listener, keeping them in suspense and releasing an emotional response with a surprising revelation. Much everyday persuasion and explanation is in the form of stories: gossip, jokes, speculation, 'war stories' or plain rumour.

Stories work best when they are concrete and personal. Tell your own, authentic stories. They will display your character and your passion. They will also be easier to remember! If you want to tell another person's story, explain that it's not yours and tell it swiftly. A story will persuade your listener if it has a clear point. Without a point, it can become counterproductive: an annoying diversion and a waste of time. You may need to make it clear: 'and the point of the story is...'.

Using metaphors

Using metaphors, as discussed in Chapter 3, is the technique of expressing one thing in terms of another. Metaphors allow you to see things in new ways by showing how they relate to others. The most persuasive metaphors make a direct appeal to the senses and to experience.

They burn ideas into your listener's mind (that's a metaphor!). They help listeners to remember by creating pictures (or sounds, or tastes, or smells) that they can store in their mind (I'm using the metaphor of a cupboard or library to explain some part of the mind's working).

REMEMBERING YOUR IDEAS

Memory played a vital role in the art of rhetoric in the days before printing. With no ready means of making notes or easy access to books, remembering ideas and their relationships was an essential skill. Whole systems of memory were invented to help people store information and recall it at will.

These days, memory hardly seems to figure as a life skill – except for passing examinations. Technology has taken its place. These's no *need* to remember: merely to read and store e-mails, pick up messages (voice and text) on the mobile, plug in, surf and download...

However, memory still plays an important part in persuading others. If you can't begin to persuade someone without a heap of spreadsheets and a briefcase full of project designs to refer to, don't start. Nobody was ever persuaded by watching someone recite from a sheaf of notes.

Find a way to bring the ideas off paper and into your head. Give yourself some clear mental signposts so that you can find your way from one idea to the next. Write a few notes on a card or on the back of your hand. Draw a mind map. Make it colourful. If you've assembled a mental pyramid, draw it on a piece of paper and carry it with you. Have some means available to draw your thoughts as you explain them: a notepad, a flip chart, a white-board. Invite the other person to join in: encourage them to think of this as the shape of *their* thinking.

DELIVERING EFFECTIVELY

Delivery means supporting your ideas with effective behaviour. Chapter 2 showed how non-verbal communication is a vital component in creating understanding. When you're seeking to persuade, your behaviour will be the most persuasive thing about you. If you're saying one thing but your body is saying another, no one will believe your words.

Think about the style of delivery your listener might prefer. Do they favour a relaxed, informal conversational style or a more formal, presentational delivery? Are they interested in the broad picture or do they want lots of supporting detail? Will they want to ask questions?

Delivery is broadly about three kinds of activity. Think about the way you use your:

- eyes;
- voice;
- body.

Effective eye contact

People speak more with their eyes than with their voice. Maintain eye contact with your listener. If you are talking to more than one person, include everybody with your eyes. Focus on their eyes: don't look through them. There are two occasions when you might break eye contact: when you are thinking about what to say next; and when you are looking at notes, a mind map or some other object of common attention.

Using your voice

Your voice will sound more persuasive if it is not too high, too fast or too thin. Work to regulate and strengthen your breathing while you speak. Breathe deep and slow. Let your voice emerge more from your body than from your throat. Slow down the pace of your voice, too: it can be all too easy to gabble when you're involved in an argument or nervous about the other person's reactions. The more body your voice has, and the more measured your vocal delivery, the more convincing you will sound.

Persuasive body language

Your face, your limbs and your body posture will all contribute to the total effect your ideas have on the listener. To start with, try not to frown. Keep your facial muscles moving and your neck muscles relaxed. Use your hands to paint pictures, to help you find the right words and express yourself fully.

Professional persuaders observe their listeners' behaviour and quietly mirror it. If you are relaxed with the other person, such mirroring will tend to happen naturally: you may find you're crossing your legs in similar ways or moving your arms in roughly the same way. Try consciously to adapt your own posture and movement to that of the person listening to you. Do more: take the lead. Don't sit back or close your body off when you are seeking to persuade; bring yourself forward, open yourself up and present yourself along with your ideas.

In brief

- We can persuade by using:
  - evidence; and
  - three modes of 'artistic' appeal.
- The three modes of 'artistic' appeal are:
  - *ethos*: appealing to our audience's sense of our character or reputation;
  - *logos*: appealing to their reason;
  - *pathos*: appealing to their emotions.

- *Ethos* is the appeal to our audience through:
  - personality
  - reputation
  - personal credibility
- *Logos* uses two forms of logic:
  - deductive
  - inductive
- *Pathos* is the appeal to emotions or feelings.
  - The pathetic appeal must always be indirect.
  - Pathos should never be dishonest.
  - Provoke the feeling that's appropriate to the action you want the audience to take.
- The *process* of working out how to persuade them consists of five key elements.
  - Identifying the core idea.
  - Arranging your ideas logically.
  - Developing an appropriate style in the language you use.
  - Remembering your ideas.
  - Delivering your ideas with words, visual cues and non-verbal behaviour.
- To identify the core idea, ask:
  - 'What is my objective?'
  - 'Who am I talking to?'
  - 'What is the most important thing I have to say to them?'

- The message sentence should be:
  - a single idea;
  - no longer than about fifteen words long;
  - action-centred;
  - self-contained; and
  - attention-grabbing.
- To arrange your ideas logically:
  - Ask what question your message provokes:
    - 'Why?'
    - 'How?'
    - 'Which ones?'
  - Use SPQR to introduce your message and fill in the background
  - Use deductive or inductive logic to arrange your supporting ideas
- To express your ideas more vividly, use:
  - images
  - examples
  - stories
  - metaphors
- To remember your material, use visual aids such as:
  - mindmaps
  - flipcharts
  - whiteboards
- And to deliver your ideas well:
  - maintain effective eye contact
  - use your voice well
  - make your body language persuasive

MAKING A PRESENTATION

Think of a presentation as a formal conversation. Speaking to groups is notoriously stressful. Conversations, after all, are natural; presentations are not. Something strange seems to happen when we're called upon to talk to a group of people formally. A host of irrational – and maybe not so irrational – fears raise their ugly heads.

What do you fear most?

A recent study in the United States asked people about their deepest fears. The results were interesting. Here they are, in order:

- speaking to groups;
- heights;
- insects and bugs;
- financial problems;
- deep water;
- sickness;
- death;
- flying;
- loneliness;
- dogs.

I think that one of the main causes of this anxiety is that you put yourself on the spot when you present. The audience will be judging, not just your ideas and your evidence, but you as well. People may not remember reports or spreadsheets easily, but they *will* remember you. If you seemed nervous, incompetent or ill-informed, that reputation will stick – at least until your next presentation.

You, the presenter, are at the heart of it. An effective presenter puts themselves centre-stage. An ineffective presenter tries to hide behind notes, a lectern, slides or computer-generated graphics. To become more effective, you need to take control of the three core elements of the event:

- the material;
- the audience;
- yourself.

Whatever you are presenting, you will also need to use all the skills of persuasion that we explored in Chapter 5:

- working out your big idea: your message;
- validating your message using SPQR (situation–problem–question–response);
- arranging your ideas coherently;
- expressing your ideas vividly;
- remembering your ideas;
- delivering effectively.

PUTTING YOURSELF ON SHOW

Think a bit more about this business of nerves. What's going on in those minutes and hours before you stand up and make your presentation? What is your body saying?

That nervous, jittery feeling is caused by adrenalin. This is a hormone secreted by your adrenal glands (near your kidneys). Adrenalin causes your arteries to constrict, which increases your blood pressure and stimulates the heart. Why stimulate the heart? To give you extra energy. When do you need extra energy? When you're in danger. Adrenalin release is an evolved response to threat.

Adrenalin has two other effects. It increases your concentration – particularly useful when making a presentation. Less usefully, adrenalin also stimulates excretion of body waste. This decreases your body weight, giving you a slight advantage when it comes to running! That's why you want to visit the toilet immediately before presenting.

Your anxiety is probably more about your relationship with the audience than about what you have to say. In the moments before you present, you may find yourself suffering from one or more of the following conditions:

- demophobia – a fear of people;
- laliophobia – a fear of speaking;
- katagelophobia – a fear of ridicule.

Check your condition against this list of adrenalin-related symptoms:

- rapid pulse;
- shallow breathing;
- muscle spasms in the throat, knees and hands;
- dry mouth;
- cold extremities;
- dilated pupils;
- sweaty palms;
- blurred vision;
- nausea.

And the worst of it is that, however much you suffer, the audience will forget virtually everything you say! That's the bad news. The good news is that you're not alone. Every presenter – indeed, every performer – suffers from nerves. Many actors and musicians talk about the horror of nerves and the fact that experience never seems to make them better.

The best news is that nerves are there to help you. They are telling you that this presentation matters – and that *you* matter. You are the medium through which the audience will understand your ideas. You *should* feel nervous. If you don't, you aren't taking the presentation seriously and you're in danger of letting your concentration slip.

PREPARING FOR THE PRESENTATION

The trick is not to try to dispel the nerves, but to use them. Once you understand that nervousness is natural, and indeed necessary, it becomes a little easier to handle.

Everyone is frightened of the unknown. Any presentation involves an element of uncertainty, because it's 'live'. You can't plan for the audience's mood on the day. You may not even be able to foresee who will be there. You can't plan for any sudden development that affects the proposal or explanation you are giving. You can't plan for every question that you might be asked. This is, of course, the greatest strength of presentations: you and the audience are together, in the same place, at the same time. You're bringing the material alive for them, here and now.

The trick is to know what to leave to chance. If you can support your nerves with solid preparation, you can channel your nervous energy into the performance itself. Prepare well, and you can bring the presentation to life.

Prepare in three areas:

1 the material;

2 the audience;

3 yourself.

In each case, preparation means taking control. If you can remove the element of uncertainty in these areas, you'll be ready to encounter what can't be controlled: the instantaneous and living relationship between you and your audience.

MANAGING THE MATERIAL

Many presentations fail, not because the presenter is weak, but because the material is disorderly. The audience gets lost. You have to remember that they'll forget virtually everything you say. They may remember rather more of what you show them, but only if it's simple. Don't expect any audience to remember, from the presentation alone, more than half a dozen ideas.

In presentations, more than in any other kind of corporate communication, you must display the shape of your thinking. That shape will only be clear if you keep it simple. Detail doesn't make things clearer; it makes things more complicated. If you want to display the shape of your thinking, you must design it. Managing the material is a design process (Figure 6.1).

Defining your objective

Why are you making this presentation? That's the first, and most important, question you must answer. Everything else – the material you include, its order, the level of detail you go into, how long the presentation will last, what visual aids you will use – will depend on your answer to this question.

What do you want your audience to take away at the end of the presentation? More importantly: what do you want them to *do*?

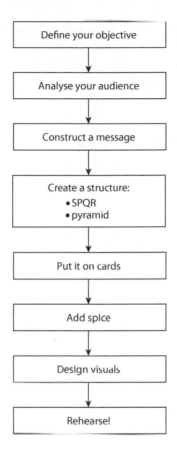

Figure 6.1 Planning a presentation

Your objective is to tell them everything they need to know to take that action – and nothing more.

Presentations are not ideal for giving information. To repeat: your audience is probably going to forget almost all the information you give them. So packing the presentation full of information is almost certainly counterproductive. If you must offer your audience detailed information, put it in supporting notes.

I believe that there's only one reason why you should be making a presentation. It may sound rather grand, but a presentation should *inspire* your audience. They want to be interested: to be moved, involved, intrigued. Your task is to bring your ideas alive with your own feelings, commitment and passion. You can demonstrate this commitment further when the audience asks questions. It's your conviction that the audience is looking for.

How many points to put across?

I think the answer should be 'one'. If the average member of the audience can remember with interest and enthusiasm one main theme, the lecture has been a great success.

(Sir Lawrence Bragg, quoted in Max Atkinson (2004), *Lend Me Your Ears*, Vermilion Press, London)

So your objective must be to inspire your audience. If you have any other objective, choose another method of communication. If you are simply making a pronouncement and not seeking or expecting any kind of response, you may as well write it down. For teaching or instructing, you will need to adapt a presentation into a much more interactive activity.

Write your objective down in one sentence. This helps you to:

- clear your mind;
- select material to fit;
- check at the end of planning that you are still addressing a single clear issue.

Write a simple sentence beginning:

'The aim of this presentation is to...'

Make sure the verb following that word 'to' is suitably inspirational!

Analysing your audience

Your presentation will be successful if the audience feels that you have spoken directly to them. If you can demonstrate that you've tailored your material to their needs, the audience will be more inclined to accept it.

So think about your audience carefully.

- How many will there be?
- What is their status range?
- Will they want to be there?
- How much do they already know about the matter? How much more do they need to know?
- What will they be expecting? What is the history, the context, the rumour, the gossip?
- How does your message and your material relate to the audience? Relevance defines what you will research, include and highlight. It will also help you to decide where to start: what your point of entry will be.
- Is the audience young or old? Are they predominantly one gender or mixed?
- Are they technical specialists or generalists? Each group will want different levels of detail.
- Where are they in the organization? Different working groups will have different interests and different ways of looking at the world.

Think, too, about the audience's expectations of the presentation. They may see presentations often, or very rarely. They may also have specific expectations of you, the presenter: they may know you well, or hardly at all; you may have some sort of reputation that goes before you.

Match or exceed your audience's expectations

Broadly, your audience has certain expectations, of you and of itself. How will you meet these, or exceed them? You may, of course, want to confound their expectations: but this may be a little risky!

Audience's expectations of you	*Audience's expectations of itself*
Set direction and pace	To be led
Be competent	To work at the speaker's pace
Know your stuff	To be told what to do (take notes, ask questions, etc)
Be confident	

Constructing a message

Once you have your objective, and some sense of who your audience is, you can begin to plan your material. Begin with a clear message. This should have all the characteristics of the messages that we looked at in Chapter 5. Your message must:

- be a sentence;

- express your objective;

- contain a single idea;

- have no more than 15 words;

- grab your audience's attention.

You might consider putting this message on to a slide or other visual aid and showing it near the start of the presentation. But an effective message should stick in the mind without any help. Make your message as vivid as you can.

Creating a structure

Everything in the structure of the presentation should support your message. Keep the structure of your presentation simple. The audience will forget most of what you say to them. Make sure that they remember your message and a few key points.

Weaving an introduction

Use SPQR to start the presentation, leading the audience from where they are to where you want them to be. This also allows you to show that you understand their situation and that you are there to help them. Using SPQR will convince them that you have put yourself into their shoes. The more obvious the problem is to the audience, the less time you will need to spend on SPQR.

SPQR also allows you to demonstrate your own credentials for being there. (Look back at the notes on *ethos* in Chapter 5.) Your values and beliefs are what make you credible to the audience: they are judging you as well as what you have to say. What qualifies you to speak on this subject? What special experience or expertise do you have? How can you add value to the ideas in your presentation?

Your own values and beliefs will be more credible if you can weave them into a story. SPQR gives you the structure. You could begin your presentation by telling a brief story, making sure that your audience will be able to relate to it. Stories have a way of sticking in the mind long after arguments have faded. Choose a story that demonstrates your values in relation to the matter in hand. Beware generalized sentiment. Make the story authentic and relevant. And keep it brief. You need to allow as much time as possible for your new ideas.

Building a pyramid

Use a pyramid structure to outline your small number of key points. Show the pyramid visually: on PowerPoint slides, or a flip chart. Indicate that these key points will form the sections of the presentation.

Repetition is an essential feature of good presentations. Because the audience can't reread or rewind to remind themselves of what you said, you need to build their recall by repeating the key features of your presentation. The key features will be your message, your structure, your key points and any call to action that you deliver at the end. Aim to build the audience's recall on no more than about half-a-dozen pieces of information.

Most people seem to know the famous *tell 'em* principle:

- Tell 'em what you're going to tell 'em.
- Tell 'em.
- Tell 'em what you've told 'em.

Build the three-part repetition into the presentation as a whole: tell 'em at the start what the whole presentation will cover; and tell 'em at the end what the whole thing has covered. Use the technique, too, within each part of the presentation: summarizing at the start and end, so that you lead the audience into and out of each section explicitly.

Don't be afraid to repeat your ideas. If you want the audience to remember them, you can't repeat them too often.

If you plan well, you'll almost certainly create too much material. You must now decide what to leave out, and what you could leave out if necessary. Be ruthless. Bear in mind that your audience will forget most of what you say. Go back to your pyramid and make sure that you have enough time to cover each key point. Weed out any detail that will slow you down or divert you from your objective.

Opening and closing the presentation

Once the body of the presentation is in place, you need to design an opening and close that will help you take off and land safely. You need to be able to perform these on 'autopilot'. Memorize them word for word, or write them out in full.

The opening of your presentation should include:

- introducing yourself – who you are and why you are there;
- acknowledging the audience – thanking them for their time and recognizing what they are expecting;
- a clear statement of your objective or, better still, your message;
- a timetable – finish times, breaks if necessary;
- rules and regulations – note-taking, how you will take questions;
- any 'housekeeping' items – safety, refreshments, administration.

Once these elements are in place, you can decide exactly how to order the items. You might decide to start with something surprising or unusual: launching into a story or a striking example, seemingly improvising some remark about the venue or immediate circumstances of your talk, asking a question. Sometimes it's a good idea to talk with the audience informally before launching into the presentation proper.

The close of the presentation is the most memorable moment. Whatever else happens, the audience will almost certainly remember this! This is your last chance to 'tell 'em what you've told 'em.' Summarize your key points, and your message. Give a call to action. Add feeling: this is the place for you to invoke *pathos*. (Look back at the start of Chapter 5 for more on this.) Be specific in your call to action: what *exactly* do you want the audience to do?

Thank the audience for their attention. You might also formally guide them into a question session, giving them time to relax after concentrating and perhaps pre-arranging a 'planted question' in the audience to set the ball rolling.

Putting it on cards

The best presentations are given without notes. But few people will always have the confidence or experience to be able to deliver without any help. Nevertheless, any notes you create should aim to support your memory, not substitute for it.

Don't write your presentation out in full unless you are an accomplished actor. Only actors can make recitation sound convincing – and nobody is asking you to act. Use cards. Filing or archive cards are best; use the largest you can find. Cards have a number of key advantages.

- They are less shaky than paper – they don't rustle.
- They are more compact.
- They give your hands something firm to hold.
- They can be tagged with a treasury tag to prevent loss of order.
- They look more professional.
- They force you to write only brief notes.

By writing only brief notes, triggers and cues on your cards, you force yourself to think about what you are saying, while you are saying it. This means that you will sound much more convincing. Obviously, your audience will only tolerate a certain amount of silence while you think of the next thing to say. The note on the card is there to trigger that next point and keep you moving.

Write your notes in bold print, using pen or felt-tip. Write on only one side and number the cards sequentially. Include:

- what you *must* say;
- what you *should* say to support the main idea;
- what you *could* say if you have time.

Add notes on timing, visual aids, and cues for your own behaviour. Keep the cards simple to look at and rehearse with them so that you get to know them.

Adding spice

Exciting presentations bring ideas alive. You are the medium through which the audience understands the material. You must make the presentation your own and give it the smell of real life.

Rack your brain for anything you can use. Think it up, cook it up, dream it up if necessary. Look for:

- images;
- examples;
- analogies;
- stories;
- pictures;
- jokes (but be very careful about these).

The aim is to create pictures in your audience's mind. Don't let computer graphics do it all for you. And don't fall into the trap of thinking that putting text on a slide makes it visual. Your audience wants *images*: real pictures, not words.

The most powerful pictures are the ones you can conjure in your audience's imagination with your own words. There's a famous story about a little girl who claimed she liked plays on the radio, 'because the pictures were better'. You should be aiming to create such pictures in your audience's mind.

Designing visuals

Working on the visuals can take longer than any other part of planning. The important thing to remember is that any aid you use is there to help you, not to substitute for you. You are *not* a voice-over accompanying a slide presentation; the pictures are there to illustrate your ideas. The audience wants to see *you*: to meet with you, assess you, ask you questions, learn about you. They will not have the chance to do any of this if you hide behind your visual aids.

Visual aids intrude. The moment you turn on the projector or turn to the flip chart, the audience's attention is on that, rather than you. A small number of excellent visual aids will have far more impact than a large number of indifferent ones. Don't fall into the trap of thinking that every part of the presentation should have an accompanying slide.

Make your visuals just that: *visual*. If you can avoid using words, do so. How can you put the information into graphic form? Is there a picture you can use to illustrate or suggest what you are saying? Words are for listening to. Visual aids are for looking at. It really is that simple.

---

6 × 6 × 6

If you *must* put words on your slides, they should obey this design principle.

No more than six lines of text on any slide.

No more than six words on any one line.

The text should be visible *on a laptop screen* from a distance of six metres. (For most fonts, this means a minimum size of about 24pt.)

Audiences' expectations of slides are changing. We all know that it's quite easy to produce slides with flashy animation. Many audiences are becoming bored with endless slide shows. Confound your audience's expectations. Use the technology by all means – and then leap away from it, galvanizing your audience with your own passion for your subject. Or be really daring, and work without any slides at all.

Rehearsing

There's a world of difference between thinking your presentation through and doing it. You may think you know what you want to say, but until you say it you don't really know. Only by uttering it aloud can you test whether you understand what you are saying. Rehearsal is the reality check.

Rehearsal is also a time check. Time acts oddly in presentations. It can seem to stop, to drag and – more often than not – to race away. The most common time problem I encounter with trainees who are rehearsing their presentations is that they run out of time. They are astounded when I tell them that time is up and they have hardly finished introducing themselves! You *must* rehearse to see how long it all takes. Be aware that it will probably take longer than you anticipate: maybe 50 per cent longer.

Rehearsing: general guidelines

- Rehearse in real time: don't skip bits.
- Rehearse with a friend. Ask them what they think and work with them to improve.
- Rehearse with your notes. Get into the habit of looking up from them.
- Rehearse with the visual aids at least once.
- Rehearse in the venue itself if you can. If you can't, try to spend some time there, getting the feel of the room.

The ultimate aim of rehearsal is to give you freedom in the presentation itself. Once you have run through the presentation a few times, you will be able to concentrate on the most important element of the event; your relationship with the audience. Under-rehearsed presenters spend too much time working out what to say. Well-rehearsed presenters know what to say and can improvise on it according to the demands of the moment.

Try to think of each presentation as brand new. After all, it's probably new for this particular audience. They haven't heard your stories or arguments before. They are going on this journey for the first time. Change the material a little each time you present. Think of a new story or a new example.

You must also rehearse with any equipment that you intend to use. Nothing is more nerve-wracking than trying to present with a projector or laptop you've never seen before.

- Talk without support. Don't use the visuals as a crib.
- Don't talk to visuals. They can't hear you. Avoid turning your back on the audience.
- Don't let the light of the visuals put you in darkness.
- Make sure you know how to put things right if they go wrong.
- If you can, be ready to present without any visual aids at all.

CONTROLLING THE AUDIENCE

Many presenters concentrate so hard on the material that they ignore the audience. They have no idea of the messages that their body is sending out. They are thinking so hard about *what* they are saying that they have no time to think about *how* they say it.

You are performing. Your whole body is involved. You must become aware of what your body is doing so that you can control it, and thus the audience.

Eye contact

Our eyes are enormously communicative. Your eyes tell the audience that you are taking notice of them, that you're confident to speak to them, that you know what you're talking about and that you believe what you're saying.

Look at the audience's eyes throughout the presentation. Imagine that a lighthouse beam is shooting out from your eyes and scanning the audience. Make sure that the beam enters every pair of eyes in the room. Focus for a few seconds on each pair of eyes and meet their gaze. Don't look past them, through them or over their heads. Pick out a few faces that look particularly friendly and return to them. After a while, you may even feel confident enough to return to a few of the less friendly ones!

Include the whole audience with your eyes. Many presenters fall into the trap of focusing on only one person: the most senior manager, the strongest personality, maybe simply someone they like a lot.

Keep your cue cards in your hand so that you can easily glance down at them and bring your eyes back to the audience quickly.

Your face

The rest of your face is important, too! Remember to smile. Animate your face and remember to make everything just a little larger than life so that your face can be 'read' at the back of the room.

Gestures

Many presenters worry about how much or little they gesture. This is reasonable. Arms and hands are prominent parts of the body and can sometimes get out of control.

The important thing is to find the gestures that are natural for you. If you're a great gesticulator, don't try to force your hands into rigid stillness. If you don't normally gesture a great deal, don't force yourself into balletic movements. Use your hands to paint pictures and to help you get the words out. Keep your gestures open, away from your body and into the room. Don't cross your hands behind your back, and don't put them in your pockets too much. (It's a good idea to empty your pockets before the presentation so that you don't find yourself jingling coins or keys.)

Movement

Aim for stillness. This doesn't mean that you should stand completely still all the time. Moving about the room shows that you're making the space your own, and helps to energize the space between you and the audience. But rhythmic, repetitive movement can be annoying and suggest the neurotic pacing of a panther in a cage. Try not to rock on your feet or tie your legs in knots! Aim to have both feet on the ground as much as possible and slow down your movements.

LOOKING AFTER YOURSELF

And you'll *still* be nervous as the moment of truth approaches. Remember that those nerves are there to help you. If you've prepared adequately, you should be ready to use your nerves to encounter the uncertainty of live performance.

You certainly need time before presenting that is quiet and focused. I need to spend about 15 minutes doing nothing but preparing myself mentally. I put myself where nothing can distract me from the presentation. Visualizing success immediately before the presentation works for some people. Ahead of time, imagine yourself presenting, the audience attentively listening to your every word, applauding you at the end and asking keen questions afterwards.

On some occasions, it can be useful to meet the audience and chat with them before you start. This can break the ice and put you more at ease.

The most important preparation involves breathing. Make contact with the deepest kind of breathing, which works from the stomach rather than the upper part of the lungs. Slow that breathing down, and make it calm, regular and strong. This works wonders for the voice: it gives it depth and power, and makes for a more convincing delivery.

Along with your breathing, pay attention to the muscles around your mouth that help you to articulate. Try some tongue-twisters or sing a favourite song. Chew the cud, and get your tongue and lips really working and warmed up. A very simple exercise is to stick your tongue as far out of your mouth as you can and then speak a part of your presentation, trying to make the consonants as clear as you can. You only need to do this for about 30 seconds to wake up your voice and make it clearer. You will, of course, look rather silly while doing this, so it's best to do the exercise in a private place!

ANSWERING QUESTIONS

Many presenters are as worried about the question session as about the presentation itself. A few guidelines can help to turn your question session from a trial into a triumph:

- *Decide when to take questions*. This will probably be at the end. But you might prefer to take questions during the presentation. This is more difficult to manage but can improve your relationship with the audience.

- *Anticipate the most likely questions*. These may be 'Frequently Asked Questions' that you can easily foresee. Others may arise from the particular circumstances of the presentation.

- *Use a 'plant'*. Ask somebody to be ready with a question to start the session off. Audiences are sometimes hesitant at the end of a presentation about breaking the atmosphere.

- *Answer concisely*. Force yourself to be brief.

- *Answer honestly*. You can withhold information, but don't lie. Someone in the audience will almost certainly see through you.

- *Take questions from the whole audience*. From all parts of the room and from different 'social areas'.

- *Answer the whole audience*. Don't let questions seduce you into private conversations. Make sure the audience has heard the question.

- *If you don't know, say so*. And promise what you'll do to answer later.

A simple format for answering a question

- Repeat the question if necessary. This helps you understand it, helps the audience to hear it and gives you time to think about your answer.
- Give a single answer. Make only one point.
- Now give one reason for your answer.
- Give an example that illustrates the point.

Of course, it may not be easy to think of all these as you spontaneously respond to a question. But if you slow down and try to think this simple format through, you will probably answer more succinctly and clearly.

In brief

- To make an effective presentation means taking control of:
  - the material
  - the audience
  - yourself
- To prepare the material:
  - define your objective
  - analyse your audience
  - construct a message
  - create a structure (SPQR; pyramid)
  - put it on cards
  - add spice
  - design visuals
  - rehearse

- To control the audience, work on:
  - eye contact
  - facial expression
  - gestures
  - movement
- To look after yourself, pay attention to:
  - breathing
  - articulation
  - a strategy of answering questions

PUTTING IT IN WRITING

Writing well is probably the most technically difficult form of communication. It requires skill, understanding and a good deal of creativity. And we're judged on the quality of our writing. It has to act as our ambassador in our absence.

We all know effective writing when we see it. It does its job clearly and quickly. It says what the writer wants to say; nothing gets in the way. Above all, effective writing gets results.

WRITING FOR RESULTS

Whenever we write a business document, we are seeking a result. That's why I prefer the term 'functional writing' to 'business writing'. Functional writing has a job to do. It has a practical purpose.

Writing well starts with choosing to write. Writing is slow and expensive; even writing an e-mail can take time. A telephone call may do the job more quickly. Writing is useful when:

- you want a permanent record;
- the information is complicated;
- you want to copy the same material to many readers.

It may be useful to write to someone who is never available to talk to, though there is no guarantee that they'll read your message among the dozens or hundreds they receive that day. Writing also carries a certain authority that a conversation may lack. A letter may get action more easily than a phone call because it looks more serious or official.

MAKING READING EASIER

Most of the advantages of conversation disappear when we write. Compared to talking and listening, writing and reading are slow and inefficient. A document isn't dynamic; it's static. Misunderstandings can easily arise. If the reader gets something wrong, you aren't there to help out. Worst of all, you can't even be sure that the reader will read the document.

Good writers try to make reading as easy as possible. Reading, after all, is hard work. We read on three levels:

- working out what the writer has to say;
- scanning sentences for complete ideas;
- reading individual words for their meaning.

To make reading easier, you must help the reader on all three levels.

The three golden rules of writing
- Make your point, then support it.
- Construct straightforward sentences.
- Use words that the reader is most likely to understand.

Generally, short words are easier to understand than long ones. But your reader will understand best the words that are *familiar* to them. If they know the jargon or the long abstract words, use them. If in doubt, use short words.

Similarly, shorter sentences are clearer than longer ones. But a page full of short sentences will have a 'scatter-gun' effect: lots of points but no connections. Sentences also work best when they're well constructed and grouped together in paragraphs.

The final golden rule is the most important. Say it first, then support it. Many of us write in a kind of 'stream of consciousness', putting one idea after another until we reach our conclusion. This gives our writing flow. But we should also be distinct, making sure that our ideas leap out at the reader and hook their attention. If you've something to say, always aim to say it as soon as possible. Then deliver the evidence that supports your idea.

WRITING STEP BY STEP

Writing is best tackled systematically. We all face the temptation to do everything at once: working out what to say, in what order, and how to say it. This is a recipe for disaster: we get confused and frustrated, and the writing that emerges is a garbled mess. Like cooking, writing is best done step by step.

Think in terms of constructing a document rather than merely writing it. This letter or document has a job to do; you must design and build it to do the job. The construction process has three steps:

- designing the document;
- writing a first draft;
- editing the draft.

Try to keep the stages separate. If you can take breaks between them, so much the better. It can also be useful to ask a colleague for help at each stage.

In this chapter, we look at these three stages and explore the key issues in each. Many of the techniques will already be familiar to you. The idea of delivering a single message, SPQR (situation–problem–question–response) and using a pyramid structure for organizing information, all have a place in writing well.

DESIGNING THE DOCUMENT

We can break planning a document into five stages:

- goal orientation;
- readership analysis;
- creating a message;
- organizing information;
- constructing an outline.

Goal orientation

Start by identifying the purpose of your document. Distinguish between the document's purpose and its subject. Whatever you're writing about, you must be clear what you want to achieve.

Make your purpose as specific as possible. Take care not to create a purpose that's inappropriate. For example, documents cannot analyse or evaluate. These are thinking processes. The document will display the product of your thinking. It can't do the thinking!

What do you want the document to do?

Try these verbs out for size.
I want this document to:

recommend	identify	respond
notify	update	summarize
announce	confirm	describe
clarify	invite	propose
compare	justify	request
explain	argue	suggest
highlight	outline	categorize

What do you want the reader to do as a result of reading the document? Functional documents demand action and deliver information to help achieve it. Identify the action you want the reader to take and you'll be better placed to provide the information that will help them take it.

What do you want the reader to do?

Here are some suggestions.
I want the reader to:

target areas for action	realign strategy
attend a meeting	approve funding
implement a plan	answer questions
provide input	complete a task
agree with me	review my proposal
choose from options	give me feedback
put something right	investigate an issue

Formalize your objective into a **function statement**. If necessary, agree this with the document's 'client', the person who has asked for it. By agreeing the document's functions, you'll know exactly what's required of you.

Function statement

I want this document to

[immediate aim]

so that

[proposed action]

Readership analysis

Your document may circulate to a wide readership. Different readers will have different expectations, priorities and levels of knowledge. Analyse the readership so that you can organize information in the document more effectively.

Managing readership expectations

Categorize your readership into *primary*, *secondary* and *tertiary* readers. The primary readership must read the document. The document is designed for them. The secondary readership might look at only part of the document. It might include your manager, who might need to authorize it before circulation but who won't act on it. The tertiary readership might include people you'll never meet but who might use the document in some unforeseen way. You will need to satisfy all of these readers. But you must design the document for the primary readership alone.

Identifying the key persuasive factors

The key persuasive factors are the most important elements in your reader's decision to believe you. They may arise from the reader's:

- background;
- priorities;
- needs or concerns;
- place in the corporate culture;
- relationship to the external environment.

Put yourself in the primary reader's position and ask: 'What would most convince me about this idea?'

Creating a message

Your document must deliver a single message.

The message is the most important element of the document. Everything else in it – the material, how it is ordered, how you present it – depends on the message.

The message is the single most important point you want to make to the reader. It's not a heading or title. Neither is it a description of what you're doing in the document. (A statement beginning 'the aim of this document is…', for example, is not a message.) The message *expresses* your purpose. Your document's message should be:

- a sentence;
- expressing a single idea;
- no longer than 15 words long;
- self-explanatory to the reader;
- action-centred.

It is critically important to check that your document's message is appropriate: to you, to the reader and to your material. In a conversation, interview or presentation, we can check that we're addressing the other person's needs, or the audience's expectations, on the spot. When we write, that interaction disappears. Many documents fail to give their readers what they want. SPQR is the only way you can check that you're producing the document that the reader will find useful.

Look back at Chapter 5 for more details about SPQR. The SPQR sequence can:

- help you validate your message;
- facilitate a conversation between writer and reader to clarify the document's message;
- form the core of an Introduction in the document.

Organizing information

In writing, more than anywhere else, communicating well is a matter of displaying the shape of your thinking. That shape is made up of ideas: the sentences you write. You must arrange those ideas into a coherent shape that the reader can see clearly.

Your reader can understand only one piece of information clearly at a time. To understand your message in more detail, they must first break it into pieces, then understand each piece in order. You must organize information, therefore, in two dimensions:

- vertically (breaking the message into pieces, grouping smaller pieces into larger ones);
- horizontally (organizing each group of pieces into an order).

Organizing information like this creates a shape that allows the reader's mind to understand complexity in the most natural way. The shape you create is a pyramid.

First- and second-stage thinking

We can imagine the process of creating the document's structure as a thinking process in two stages. We've looked at the two stages of thinking already as a way of structuring our conversations

(Chapter 3). Now we can use them to help us organize material for a document:

- *first-stage thinking:* gathering information;
- *second-stage thinking:* organizing the information.

Use mindmaps to help you gather information, and the pyramid principle to help you organize the information into a coherent structure.

Summarizing and grouping

Imagine speaking your message to the reader. What question will it provoke in their mind? The question should be one of three:

- 'Why?'
- 'How?'
- 'Which ones?'

You must have at least two answers to the question. Try to have no more than six. Write your answers to that question as key points. All your key points must be sentences. You should be able to align each key point to a group of ideas on your mindmap.

Creating key points

Your key points should all be of the same kind.

'Why?'	Reasons, benefits, causes
'How?'	Procedures, process steps
'Which ones?'	Items, categories, factors

For each key point, ask what question it provokes: 'Why?', 'How?' or 'Which ones?' Identify the answers to that question and write these as sub-points. Repeat if necessary for each sub-point to create minor points. For every question, you must have more than one answer.

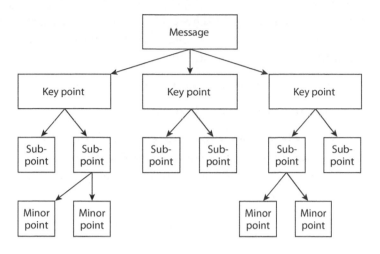

Figure 7.1 Building a pyramid

Building the pyramid

The result of this question-and-answer process is a pyramid structure (Figure 7.1).

Building pyramids: essential principles

- Every idea must be a sentence.
- Each idea must summarize the ideas grouped beneath it.
- Each idea within a group is an answer to the question provoked by the summarizing idea.

Managing detail

Building a pyramid creates a discipline that allows you to work out how much information to include in your document and how to order it.

Pyramid building always proceeds by division. Each idea provokes a question to which you must have at least two answers – and preferably not more than six. This process of division by question and answer continues until an idea fails to provoke a question with multiple answers. It can stop if:

- an idea does not provoke a question from the reader;
- an idea provokes a question that has only one answer.

It should never be necessary to create a pyramid containing more than four levels: message, key point, sub-point, minor point.

You must decide how to order ideas in each group. You can order ideas in terms of:

- rank (size, importance, priority, relevance);
- process steps;
- chronology;
- logical reasoning.

Sometimes the order of ideas is not critical.

Constructing an outline

The final stage of planning your document is constructing an outline. This transforms your pyramid into text that you can expand into a first draft.

An outline is the design of your document. It gives an overview of the entire document in miniature. Here's how to write an outline.

- At the top of a page, write your message sentence, headed *Message*.
- Follow this with a headed *Introduction*: SPQR, briefly stated (three or four lines at most).
- Write each key point sentence, numbered, in order, with each sub-point and minor point numbered beneath each key point. Use a decimal numbering system for maximum clarity:
  - 1.
  - 1.1
  - 1.1.1 and so on.

- Add a title for the whole outline, and headings for each key point, if necessary.

Once you understand this principle of creating an outline, you can adapt it to any kind of document. We'll look here at three basic formats: e-mail or memo, letter and report. You'll see that the pyramid remains the same in each case, with only slight variations.

Outlining an e-mail or memo

This is the simplest kind of pyramid.

Simply place your message at the top, immediately after your salutation. Create a short paragraph – or even a simple bullet point – for each key point, and end, if necessary, with a call to action: the next step you want the reader to take.

It's an excellent idea to compress your message into the subject line of the e-mail so that your message appears on the reader's inbox menu.

E-mail has become a standard mode of communicating in organizations. It's fast, cheap and easy to use. But in many organizations, e-mail is rapidly becoming the problem rather than the solution. Four factors seem to be contributing to this impending crisis:

- *Information overload.* A recent survey suggested that managers receive an average of 178 e-mails a day. Getting yours noticed may be the biggest problem in getting it read.

- *More haste, less understanding.* We often write e-mails so quickly that we fail to consider whether the text is comprehensible.

- *Overflowing inboxes.* When was the last time you weeded your inbox?

E-mail is writing. Treat it as you would any other kind of writing. Plan, write, edit. Here are 10 more tips to help e-mail work better for you:

1 *Make your message clear.*
2 *Minimize information.* Don't make the reader scroll down.

3 *Put the message in the subject line.* It's much more useful to have a headline-style message in this line than a heading.

4 *Don't shout.* Avoid capital letters, underlining and bold. Above all, avoid facetious or all-purpose headings such as 'Urgent' or 'Read this now!'

5 *Don't fan 'flames'.* Don't write anything in an e-mail that you wouldn't say face to face.

6 *Avoid emoticons.* Don't use symbols or silly abbreviations. Use English.

7 *Edit before sending.* E-mail is so fast that you can easily spend a few moments checking sense, spelling and punctuation.

8 *Remember that e-mail is public.* Most e-mail can be accessed on central servers. Never write anything that a lawyer might use against you.

9 *Don't spam.* Send only messages that you must send, to the individuals who need to read them. Avoid blanket copies.

10 *Clear your inbox regularly.* You'll make the system – and yourself – work much more efficiently.

Outline of an e-mail

Re: conference meeting, 2 April: key issues

Derek
There are three key issues I'd like to discuss at our meeting on Friday.

- How can we promote the conference more effectively abroad?
- How can we align the main speakers' messages effectively to support corporate strategy?
- Do we have the resources to create an informal exhibition area in the foyer?

If you have any other issues to raise, copy me in. See you there!
Gloria

Outlining a letter

The pyramid here is framed by handshakes: one at the start, and possibly one at the end. The style of a letter may differ slightly from that of an e-mail (more on style later), but apart from that, and a few other formalities of layout, the two are similar.

Outline of a letter

25 January 2014   [company logo]
Sidney Reader
Readership House
READERTOWN
AB1 2CD

Dear Sidney

Thank you for your letter of 20 January.   [*handshake*]

This is my main message.   [*message sentence*]

My first point is here.   [*paragraphs*]

...

My second point is here.

...

The next step is   [*action point*]

I hope this is satisfactory.   [*closing handshake*]

Yours sincerely

Alan Writer
[Job title]

Outlining a report

Reports tend to need the fullest kind of outline, complete with summary, introduction, numbered points and an array of sub-points and minor points.

Creating the outline is a really useful stage in constructing a report. You can use the outline to check with the report's 'client' that it is developing as they would wish, to make changes to your report without having to rewrite lots of text, and to establish that you know exactly what your key ideas are for each section. The outline can itself form the summary of the report. It will also be invaluable for those readers who only want reports that cover a single sheet of A4. For them, the outline *is* the report.

Outline of a report

Message

We should locate new plant in Gatheringham.

Introduction

Our business is rapidly expanding. Existing manufacturing plant will reach capacity within three years. We urgently need to decide where to locate new manufacturing plant. This document summarizes the findings of the relocation project and justifies its recommendation in strategic terms.

1 Capital costs in Gatheringham are estimated at 10 per cent below those of the next best location.

    1.1 Constructors' bids in the area average 10 per cent below those in other locations.

    1.2 Land costs are on average 13 per cent lower than in other areas.

---

2 Operating costs in Gatheringham are estimated to be 15 per cent lower than in other areas.

   2.1 Labour costs are 7 per cent less than the national average.

   2.2 Overheads are estimated at 9 per cent less than in current plants.

   2.3 Tax incentives for operating in this zone are very attractive.

3 Distribution costs would decrease by at least 7 per cent if centred on Gatheringham.

   3.1 The area is centrally located for our markets.

   3.2 The local infrastructure is well developed.

WRITING A FIRST DRAFT

Writing the document should be considerably easier now that the outline is complete. Essentially, you need to expand the outline by adding text, headings, and – for reports in particular – numbering and graphics. The plan of the outline is in place, and the sentences in the outline give you a clear idea of what you want to say in each paragraph and section.

Think of writing the first draft of your document as a separate activity from either planning or editing.

- *Write quickly*. Don't ponder over words. Keep going. Leave gaps if necessary. Aim for a natural flow.

- *Write in your own voice*. Expressing yourself in your own way will help you to say what you mean more exactly. If your reader can 'hear' your voice, reading will be easier.

- *Write without interruption*. Try to find a time and place where you can think and write without distractions.

- *Write without editing.* Don't try to get it right first time. Resist the temptation to edit as you go. You'll tend to get stuck and waste time.

- *Keep to the plan of your outline.* Use the sentences from your outline to focus what you want to say. If you find yourself wandering from the point, stop and move on to the next sentence in the outline.

Navigation aids

An effective document contains navigation aids to help the reader find their way around. The most important navigation aids are:

- a summary;
- an introduction;
- headings;
- bullet points.

All of these elements will help you 'sell' the document to your reader.

Summaries and introductions

Don't confuse these two essential items.

The *summary* is the document in miniature. At its heart is your message. Place the summary at the very start of the document – immediately following the title page. Your outline is a ready-made summary.

An *introduction* explains how the document came into being. At its heart is SPQR: background information including the problem addressed by the document and the question it answers. Introductions might expand to include:

- methodology;
- acknowledgements;
- a short guide to the document, section by section.

Use summaries elsewhere in the document to deliver the shape of the material – most importantly, at the start of each section.

Headings

Pay close attention to the title and other headings in your document. They should have high scanning value: the reader should be able to glean a lot of information from relatively few words. 'Financial review', for example, has low scanning value. 'Breakdown of operating costs 2013' works rather better.

Headings should be informative without being too detailed. In a report, you might assemble your headings into a contents list. Check it to see that the headings give a fair idea of content and aren't repetitious.

Bullet points

Bullet points are visually very powerful. Don't overuse them.

- Construct the points in parallel. All items should be grammatically of the same kind.
- Make the points consistent with the 'platform': the text that introduces the list.
- Improve the 'platform' so that repeated elements in the list need be expressed only once.

EFFECTIVE EDITING

The aim of editing is to make the first draft easier to read.

Editing is about making choices. It is potentially endless because there's always more than one way to say what you mean. It's especially difficult to edit your own work. Ask a colleague to help you if you can. Try to cultivate an innocent eye. Take a break before editing so that you're better prepared to look at the text afresh.

Edit systematically. Editing word by word is time-consuming and may be counterproductive. To edit efficiently, work on three separate levels in this order:

- paragraphs;
- sentences;
- words.

It's probably best to edit hard copy, rather than on screen.

Creating effective paragraphs

Paragraphs display the shape of your thinking. They show the individual main ideas and the relationships between them. Every time you make a new point, start a new paragraph.

Use a topic sentence at the start of each paragraph to summarize it. Topic sentences help you to decide what to include in each paragraph. You can think of a topic sentence as the paragraph's message. It should:

- be a fully grammatical sentence;
- make a single point;
- contain no more than 15 words;
- say something new.

An outline, of course, is a ready source of topic sentences. Another place to look for potential topic sentences is at the end of a paragraph. Very often we put the most important idea as the paragraph's conclusion. Try flipping that conclusion to the start of the paragraph as a topic sentence. Topic sentences should make sense in order. You should be able to read all the topic sentences and understand a section in summary.

Editing a paragraph

To minimize potential downtime and operational risk, it is recommended that the business case for the purchase of a back-up server, which could also be used for system testing, be formally examined. We are now addressing this since a decision is needed by the end of March to avoid additional hire costs or the loss of the rented machine.

Note how a topic sentence allows the writer to cut down the paragraph considerably and improve readability.

We are now examining the business case for buying a back-up server. This could:

- *minimize potential down-time;*
- *minimize operational risk;*
- *also be used for system testing.*

A decision is needed by the end of March to avoid extra hire costs or the loss of the rented machine.

Sentence construction

Sentences express ideas. They will express your ideas more strongly if they are constructed sturdily. Sentences are weaker when they are too long or poorly built. Aim always in your sentences to say what you mean *and no more*.

Follow the '15–25' rule. Message sentences, topic sentences and other sentences expressing big ideas should never exceed 15 words. All other sentences should be no more than 25 words long.

Strengthen sentences by:

- cutting up long sentences into shorter, separate sentences;
- simplifying complicated sentences;
- finding strong subjects and verbs.

Put the subject as close to the start of the sentence as you can, and follow it as closely as possible with its verb. Tell the reader who or what is acting in each sentence and what the actor is doing. Avoid starting sentences with *it is, there is* or *there are*. Replace weak verbs like *to be* or *to have*, or indirect verbs like *allow, ensure, let, can* or *enable*.

Editing a long sentence

It was originally planned that data conversion and implementation across the remaining business areas would follow at the end of September 2013, but following a variety of problems, considerable scope drift, changes of personnel on the project team and several amendments to the timetable, conversion did not take place until 1 April 2014 and some users were still using parts of the old system until it was finally disconnected in July 2014.

This is easily improved by cutting the sentence at the conjunctions – but, and – and using a vertical list:

The project team originally planned to convert data and implement the system in remaining business areas at the end of September 2013. However, conversion was delayed by changes in:

- *the scope of the project;*
- *personnel on the project team;*
- *the timetable.*

The system was finally converted on 1 April 2014. Some users continued to use parts of the old system until it was disconnected in July 2014.

Editing words

English has a huge vocabulary. One of the main reasons is that the language is a hybrid; many ideas can be expressed with two or three words. Maybe for this reason more than any other, plain English has grown up as a way of helping us to choose the best words for our needs.

Plain English helps any reader to understand at first reading. It tells the truth without embellishment. It is a code of practice, not a set of rigid rules.

Plain English: essential guidelines

- Make your average sentence length 15 to 20 words.
- Use only the words that your reader is most likely to understand.
- Use only as many words as you need.
- Use the strongest, clearest and most specific verbs you can.
- Say what you mean. Be positive; avoid standard expressions and tired formulas.
- Punctuate clearly and simply.

Managing vocabulary

Some words are less easily understandable than others. Pay attention in particular to:

- passive verbs;
- abstract nouns;
- unnecessary words.

Passive verbs

Verbs can be either active or passive. An active verb expresses what its subject does; a passive verb expresses what its subject suffers. Sentences with active verbs are shorter, stronger and more dynamic than those with passive ones.

*It is **anticipated that** additional disk space **may** be needed.*

We anticipate that the system will need additional disk space.

Abstract nouns

Nouns name things, people, times, places or qualities. *Concrete nouns* name things physically present in the world (*table, woman, pen, car, tree*); *abstract nouns* name ideas, concepts or qualities that cannot be sensed physically (*growth, awareness, training, marketing, possibility*).

Try to cut down your use of abstract nouns. Replace them, if you can, with verbs or adjectives. If you can replace an abstract noun only with a group of shorter, more concrete words, consider keeping it.

*There were some **differences in configuration** between the two machines which added a **degree** of **complexity** to the exercise.*

The two machines were configured differently, making the exercise more complex.

Unnecessary words

Some words contribute nothing to meaning. You might use them because they sound good, or because you don't know what to say next. Remove them.

The benefits of this arrangement are a saving in consultancy costs and the opportunity for new users to learn the system in a meaningful situation at the same time as they learn their jobs.

This arrangement saves consultancy costs and allows new users to learn the system as part of on-the-job learning.

Developing a readable style

Good writing comes alive in your mind. Nothing comes between the writer and your understanding. Effective writing is transparent.

Bringing your own writing to life is a long-term project. Here are some guidelines to point you in the right direction:

- say what you mean;
- be specific;
- be positive;
- remove blockages.

Style is personal. Choosing how to write is like choosing how to dress. Improving your writing style is not unlike improving your dress sense. Look around; imitate what you admire; aim for functional elegance rather than excessive flamboyance.

Say what you mean

Concentrate on what you want to say, not how to say it. Imagine the reader's response. If you only had a few seconds to get your point across, what would you say? Be sincere, and avoid 'scaffolding': any writing that refers to the fact that you are writing ('In this report, I shall…').

Be specific

Aim to be precise rather than vague. Avoid generalizing. Use numbers (sparingly), and names, so that your writing becomes more personal. Use verbs with a specific meaning and avoid verbs that don't mean much (*get, carry out, perform, give, conduct, implement, move, do*). Make it concrete. Give real examples. And use jargon carefully.

Be positive

The best functional writing is forward-looking and action-centred. Avoid writing too much about what has happened, what hasn't happened, what should have happened or what is wrong. Instead, write about proposals, future action and what you are doing. Make definite promises and avoid emotive language.

Remove blockages

Good writing flows like water in a pipe. The words should be under pressure. Remove blockages so that the meaning flows freely. Wherever you can, transform passive verbs into active ones, and abstract nouns into concrete ones. Remove unnecessary words and exterminate clichés. Punctuate inflated language and connect your sentences together carefully.

WRITING FOR THE WEB

Writing for the web is in many ways like writing for any other medium. A number of key features, however, make reading on screen a different experience from reading on paper. Understanding those features will help you produce more usable text for websites and web-based documents.

Key qualities of web text

Research suggests that web users feel happiest when web text is concise, scannable and objective. 'Concise' means that the text says what it needs to say and no more. 'Scannable' means that big ideas are prominent; that paragraphs are not too long; and that key words are easy to pick out. 'Objective' means that the writer tends to remove their own feelings from the text. Readers want objectivity when they are using the web; opinions and feelings tend to get in the way.

Additionally, readers have voted for:

- clear navigation aids;
- evidence of the writer's credibility;
- an informal style.

Thinking about your readers

The key to effective web-writing is to think of your reader as a visitor, rather than a long-term associate. Reading a book or a report requires a level of commitment from your reader that web reading simply doesn't demand.

Different types of visitors want different things from the web pages they visit.

- *Viewers* stay on the page for no more than a few seconds.
- *Users* want to do something (such as buying a product or registering for a web community) or find practical information.
- *Readers* are willing to browse – and actually read what they find.

Designing and writing web pages is a matter of satisfying as many of these types of visitor as you can. It's worth remembering a slogan invented by one enterprising web-writer: *'shut the door, they're coming over the fence'*. In other words, visitors to your page could be coming from anywhere: a home page, a search engine or a link from another page in a completely different part of cyberspace.

Chunking and stacking

Chunk and stack your material to satisfy the needs of viewers, users and readers. Chunking and stacking is a variation on summarizing and grouping, the structural technique we looked at earlier in this chapter.

- Chunking means breaking information into manageable, screen-sized pieces.
- Stacking means grouping the chunks into categories.

Chunking and stacking layers the material. Readers can see everything that is on the site easily and go into as much detail as they want.

Additionally, most web pages will benefit from these features.

- *Create a heading* that tells you where you are at once.
- *Write a message sentence.* We've met messages before – and this message is just like the messages you can create in any other document.
- *Provide supporting information* in fewer than 100 words per paragraph.
- *Create hyperlinks* to other pages. No page should be without a hyperlink to take you somewhere else – even if it's only back to the front page or home page.

Cues for action

Cues for action keep viewers from running away, help users to do what they want to do and encourage readers to explore the page further.

There are various actions you might want your reader to take. For example, you might want them to:

- search for information;
- contribute to a discussion forum;
- buy something;
- contact someone;
- move to another page.

Explain explicitly what action readers can take. Whatever you want them to do, make sure that you keep the action simple: as few clicks as possible, with the most basic instructions.

Always write as if you are talking directly to readers, using the word 'you'. And provide an incentive for taking the action. The incentive doesn't have to be financial! Simply telling readers what information they'll find when they click may be enough.

Cues for action: a few ideas

Click <u>here</u> to find out more about Malaysian bug creepers.

Fill out this <u>form</u> for regular updates on Paradise Project activities.

For help with elderly or disabled visitors, <u>send</u> us your telephone number and we'll contact you 24 hours before your arrival to discuss your requirements.

Take part in our northern tundra <u>quiz</u> and play for some great prizes!

You can make a difference. Sign our <u>petition</u> to save the Mexican fly-eating orchid.

Hyperlinks

Hyperlinks are a powerful innovation. Unlike conventional headings, they perform two functions: helping the reader to find their way around and acting as the transport to get them there. Hyperlinks might be:

- keywords in the text;
- names in the text;
- instructions: 'Go to the semi-tropical zone'.

Headings are the most important candidates for hyperlinks. They should act like departure and arrival signs in an airport – telling readers where to go and announcing when they have arrived.

Hyperlinks can often use blurb to give just a little detail of what the heading is promising – and encouraging the reader to go there.

Making it brief

Once you have made your web pages scannable and objective, you need to make them brief. Work at three levels: paragraph, sentence and word.

Keep a complete piece of text within one screen. Summarize, create short paragraphs of no more than about 100 words and use topic sentences – maybe in bold – at the start of each paragraph, to act as scannable summaries.

Use lists wherever you can. They can of course be lists of hyperlinks to help readers navigate more easily.

Sentence construction is as important as sentence length. Make sure that your sentences are as simple as you can make them: avoid complicated clusters of ideas, passive verbs and redundant expressions. Generally, try to keep your sentence length to no more than 25 words, or about two lines of text.

Always write in standard, plain English. You're writing for a global audience. Avoid marketing hype, promotional jargon and the language of advertising.

Making it look good

Keep the visual elements of your document simple. Use a designer if you can.

Make your print readable. Sans serif fonts (such as Arial, Verdana, Tahoma or Univers) are generally easier to read on screen than serif fonts such as Times New Roman. Use at least 12pt font and higher if possible.

Avoid too much highlighting (and never use underlining except for links). Don't use too many colours (and never use blue, red or purple except for links). And create columns no more than half a screen wide. They're easier to scan than text that spreads the full width of the screen.

Transforming conventional documents into web pages

Sometimes, you'll want to put traditionally produced documents onto a website as archive documents. Take the opportunity to make them 'web-friendly'. A few simple design features can make all the difference.

Create a summary at the head of the document – no longer than half a screen long. List the section headings at the head of the document. Create links within the document. Obvious candidates for links are the headings in your list at the top of the document. Another useful link is a permanent link to the top of the document. Make the title and main headings visible within the opening screen – not just on the opening printed page.

In brief

- The three golden rules of writing
  - Make your point, then support it.
  - Construct straightforward sentences.
  - Use words that the reader is most likely to understand.

- Produce a document in three stages:
  - designing the document
  - writing a first draft
  - editing the draft

- Designing the document involves:
  - goal orientation
  - readership analysis
  - creating a message
  - organizing information
  - constructing an outline

- When drafting, write:
  - quickly
  - in your own voice
  - without interruption
  - without editing
  - keeping to the plan of your outline

- If necessary, add navigation aids:
  - a summary
  - an introduction
  - headings
  - bullet points

- Edit on three levels:
  - paragraphs
  - sentences
  - words

- It's probably best to edit hard copy, rather than on screen.
- To develop a more readable style:
  - say what you mean
  - be specific
  - be positive
  - remove blockages
- When writing for the web, create:
  - cues for action
  - chunks and stacks
  - hyperlinks

NETWORKING: THE NEW CONVERSATION

Networking is a new name for an old idea. The word may make us cringe; but, increasingly, many of us recognize that networking is an essential part of business. A survey by Common Purpose in 2008 found that 68 per cent of business leaders expected their networking activity to increase over the next five years. The number rose to 75 per cent among the younger business leaders, between 25 and 44 years old.

Perhaps the word has a bad reputation because people misunderstand what networking is – or should be. Networking is *not*:

- selling;
- using other people for your own gain;
- putting people on the spot.

Effective networkers understand that none of us can accomplish our goals alone; that we need others to fulfil our ambitions and dreams. We're all part of communities that contribute to our well-being. Networking is a tool to help us create those communities.

> Networking is the art of building and sustaining mutually beneficial relationships.

It's through the relationships we build that we reap the benefits of networking. We can find new resources and new information; we can find help in moving forward in our career. We can find new ways to make a contribution.

Networking can be strategic or spontaneous. Strategic networking is planned; spontaneous networking happens by chance. At its best, strategic networking prepares us for the spontaneous moments of discovery.

TO NETWORK OR NOT TO NETWORK?

Networking is both a very old idea and a very new one. John Donne wrote 'No man is an island' in 1624; but the language of social networking has only begun to appear in the last 60 years or so. According to the *Oxford English Dictionary*, the word 'network' – meaning an interconnected group of people – first appeared in 1946. The words 'networker' and 'networking', referring to the activities of such groups, don't appear in print until 1976.

In 1980, Mary-Scott Welch published *Networking: The Great New Way for Women to Get Ahead*. Written, according to her obituary in *The New York Times*, 'in an era when more women were competing for jobs traditionally dominated by men', *Networking* also included the first recorded use of the word 'network' as a verb: 'this book', wrote Ms Welch, 'will show you how to network'.

Networking as a business activity was thus associated from the start with feminism. Perhaps its development is associated with a less masculine, less individualist, approach to business, in which cooperation takes precedence over competition.

What makes networking effective

Effective networking relies on three key qualities:

- an 'abundance mentality';
- generosity;
- reciprocity.

Cultivating an 'abundance mentality'

People with a 'scarcity mentality' have difficulty sharing, because they feel that holding on to their resources – property, knowledge, relationships – is vital to their success. People with an 'abundance mentality' understand that human resources – knowledge, intelligence, imagination – produce more when they are shared.

Scarcity and abundance

Scarcity mentality

- Victory means success at someone else's expense.
- Someone else's success means we have missed an opportunity.
- There are two ways to do it: my way, and your way. My way is the right way.
- Everyone is out for themselves.

Abundance mentality

- Victory means success bringing mutual benefits to all.
- The possibilities of growth and development are unlimited and common to all.
- There are three ways of doing it: my way, your way and a better way.
- Everyone has something unique to offer.

An 'abundance mentality' needs to be cultivated. We have to work at it. It's easy to slip into the scarcity mentality. Developing an abundance mentality means sacrificing something of our own: power, security, certainty. But the benefits are enormous: an abundance mentality can make us less fearful and more confident.

Being generous

With an abundance mentality, we find it easier to give unconditionally. We can give attention to others; and, as we have seen in Chapter 4, attention is at the heart of effective listening. We can also give information more easily and less egotistically.

Fostering reciprocity

Reciprocity is the recognition that none of us can survive without the help of others. All human relationships are based on the idea of give and take; networking's success depends critically on reciprocity. Humans seem to be 'hard-wired' for reciprocity; if I give you something, you will almost certainly feel obliged to offer me something in return. Because human achievements rely on cooperation, we need to find ways of trusting each other; and reciprocity provides the currency of trust. My gift to you demonstrates that you can trust me, and is an invitation to you to offer something in return, so that I can begin to trust you.

PREPARING TO NETWORK

As with any other communication skill, strategic networking tends to work better when we're well prepared. Effective networkers know why they're at a networking event. They know what they want to achieve. Networking can be exhausting, so having a plan will help you evaluate your success and decide when you can take a rest.

Preparing yourself

Networking puts us on the spot. However politely we skirt around the subject, the first thing we want to know about someone is who they are: not just a name, but an identity. We are looking for something we can relate to, something we can recognize and feel comfortable with. Whether we're the first to offer the information, or the first to enquire, it helps if we have a clear 'script' that we can draw on to present ourselves clearly and easily to others.

Build your brand

Our brand is what others know us to be. It is not our personality, or our mission in life. It's closer to reputation, but more immediate. Our brand is the message we want to give others about ourselves.

Think of your brand as sitting 'on the surface'. Other qualities sit below the surface: your beliefs, values, attitudes. You don't need to display them, you may not want to display them and it may be inappropriate to display them. But your brand suggests them.

Finding your core values

1 What matters to you?
2 If you didn't have to work, what would you do?
3 What puts you 'in the zone'?
4 What big problems would you like to do something about?
5 What do you admire in others?
6 What would you like people to say about you at your 75th birthday party?
7 Who are your heroes?
8 What's the one thing about yourself you would most like to change?
9 What makes you proud about yourself?
10 What makes you different from everybody else?

Our values find expression in our accomplishments. Accomplishments are instant talking points, opening up new possibilities for conversation; they're evidence of experience and expertise that others might be looking for; they signal values to others without the need to spell them out.

It's not always easy to remember everything we've achieved, and it's not always obvious how our accomplishments might help others. If you make a list of your accomplishments, they'll be ready in the background for you to use.

Expertise and accomplishments: a checklist

Make a note of what you are:	*– and how these skills have helped you accomplish:*
good at	work projects
experienced with	sports activities
trained in	educational or training courses
natural with	family or relationship successes
successful in	volunteering or community work

It's up to you to acknowledge and celebrate your accomplishments. After all, only you know what they are! And when you start to talk about what you've achieved, you'll begin to speak with passion about something you care about: always an infectious pleasure in conversation.

Create a self-introduction

We introduce ourselves to others so often that it's worth thinking about how to do it well. A self-introduction that develops rapport and generates interest can be one of our greatest networking assets.

Develop a self-introduction that you feel comfortable with. Practise different forms of words and see which ones trigger interest and intrigue. Which ones express your 'brand': your values and attitudes, as well as what you do?

Your self-introduction: a checklist

Keep it short	Your self-introduction should take no more than five seconds. Find the headline that summarizes what you do in a single sentence.
Use a verb	State what you do – not what you are. Your introduction will be more dynamic and less ambiguous. 'I specialize in minor injuries at an A&E unit' is much more interesting than 'I'm a nurse'. 'I run training courses in communication skills' resolves the ambiguity of 'I'm a trainer'.
Be distinctive	What marks you out from others? What's different about what you do? What's unusual about the way you do business? What is the thing you really like doing?
Provide hooks	Use familiar language, not jargon or technical terms. Talk about what you do in terms of how other people experience it. Above all, keep using verbs: those 'doing' words will bring you alive in the other person's mind.
Engage	Beware the temptation to apologize for your existence! Smile; use clear and steady eye-contact; avoid words like 'just' and 'only' ('I'm just a secretary'; 'I'm only here because my manager asked me to come'). People will remember your warmth, your energy and your behaviour more than the words you use. Practise in front of a mirror, or with a friend. Do you look as if you mean what you are saying?

Many of us find it uncomfortable to 'blow our own trumpet'. But we don't need to play loudly or boisterously! People need to know what you have to offer, so that they can call on your talents. Quiet confidence and self-assurance are often more effective than blatant advertising.

Practice makes perfect. Practise being confident and professional; think about how to display your enthusiasm and energy. Try out your self-introduction at every opportunity. Ask trusted colleagues how you're doing. You are your own best public relations consultant. You know what you have to offer, and how good it is. You need to make it visible.

Marshal your resources

As with any other kind of communication, we have resources in three major areas that can help us. *Visual* resources include how we look and behave; our *vocal* resources are our voice and the parts of our body that support voice production; and *verbal* resources are the words we use.

If you marshal these resources *before* the event, you'll be better placed to use them during the event.

Visual resources

If you want to be perceived as professional, then you'll need to look professional and behave professionally.

- *Think about your wardrobe.* Build a clothes collection that represents your own values elegantly and simply. Buy a few, good-quality outfits that you can mix and match, rather than a lot of inferior-quality clothes. Darker colours generally work better than lighter shades: they hide stains and flatter the figure more effectively; and they tend to give an air of authority. If in doubt, dress *up* for the occasion; it's easy to adjust being over-dressed, but there's not much we can do on the spot to make up for being underdressed.

- *Use accessories wisely.* Learn how the extras can pull your image together. Jewellery, ties, scarves, bags, cases – they may project your brand more powerfully than your clothes. Coordination is key. A mix 'n' match approach may suggest the image of a scatterbrain.

- *Pay attention to grooming.* The state of your shoes, nails and hair matter. You're meeting people close up. It's worth thinking even about your breath.

- *Mind your manners.* How you stand, move and make eye contact: all say something about you. Pay attention to posture. The best thing you can wear is a smile.

Looks matter; and looking good is a mark of respect to the people you're meeting.

Vocal resources

The quality of your voice is also important. Volume, pace and pitch are the three core elements of our voice; we instinctively read a great deal about a person from our perceptions of these three vocal dimensions.

- *Make yourself heard.* You will probably be speaking against a babble of other voices. Direct your voice clearly at the other person; if they look as if they are straining to hear you, help by raising the volume a little.

- *Slow down.* Articulate clearly and don't gabble. Rushing your words will indicate nervousness or lack of interest. Use the breathing techniques mentioned in Chapter 6.

- *Lower your tone.* A thin, high-pitched voice will suggest a lack of authority or confidence. It's not easy to alter the tone of your voice convincingly; but if you breathe deeply and evenly, and feel your voice rising from the centre of your body rather than from a constricted throat, your tone will acquire strength and – well, body! Beware also the irritating habit of 'uptalk': the creeping tendency to end explanatory sentences on an upward inflection, as if asking a question. (Its fancy name is the 'high-rising terminal'.)

- *Use your own accent.* Trying to fake a voice that is not yours, or to alter your natural voice, is unnecessary. Be proud of your voice: it is a vital component of your identity. If your accent is distinct or strong, people may have to work a little harder to adjust to your voice.

- *Speak clearly.* Make sure all the consonants are clear when you are speaking (all the letters that are not A, E, I, O or U). Use your lips and tongue well.

As with our other resources, we need to prepare our voice to perform well. Practise in friendly situations; check how you're doing with colleagues and friends whose opinion you trust.

Verbal resources

Among your verbal resources are your self-introduction and the rapport-building remarks and questions. Listen, also, for the words the other person is using and adjust your vocabulary to theirs. Echoing the actual words a person uses can help to build rapport very quickly, if done subtly.

Do you have a card?

Your business card is the trace you leave behind you. Its job is to represent you in someone's memory after you've finished talking. If they want to meet you again, your card is the means by which they do it.

- *The card should reflect your 'brand'.* Does the design say what you want it to say? Do the colours and typefaces suggest your values and style? Are they compatible with your website or blog, if you have one?

- *Essential information should be easy to see.* Your name, your company and the contact details should leap off the card.
- *Make use of space.* Don't clutter the card with unnecessary pictures or design features.
- *Quality pays.* Choose durable, good-quality card. It's almost certainly worth having your card printed professionally, if you can afford it.

If you're new to the job market, or between jobs, take the trouble to create a new card containing your contact details. Handing out a card with outdated information is not a good idea – and makes an even worse impression if the information is hastily crossed out or overwritten. You may feel uncomfortable offering a stranger your address; a telephone number and e-mail address is quite sufficient.

Card games

Business cards can do more than represent you. They can themselves become sources of conversation.

What about the reverse of the card? It might be a useful place to put a slogan that develops your brand or style. You could leave it blank, or ruled with discreet lines, to encourage people to make notes about your conversation.

Have a supply of blank cards. They're useful for jotting down vital information (having a pen at the ready is a good idea, too!). You can use them yourself, and offer them to hapless contacts who find themselves without the necessary equipment to make notes.

Decide how to store your cards. A cardholder looks more professional than a wad of cards in your breast pocket. A fancy cardholder can also be a talking point. Some people even carry two cardholders: one for their own cards, the other for cards they receive. People might be impressed to see their cards being stowed carefully in an elegant case.

How about a souvenir card? This is a card, exactly the same size as a business card, containing useful information relating to your business or work. An IT consultant might provide a card with little-known, instant computer fixes; a trainer might offer top tips for a key area they train. Souvenir cards make you more memorable; they build your brand; and they act as instant free gifts. They might even trigger a subliminal reciprocal response.

Look after your inner self

And it can still be hard work. Networking is exhausting and can be debilitating. After all, most of us meet a few new people every day; but few of us would find it entirely natural to meet dozens of new people in a couple of hours. Every new meeting is an opportunity, but it's also a challenge. We all need to look after ourselves before submitting to the next networking event.

Building up your confidence

However well we prepare, we may still lack the confidence to enter a room full of strangers. To counter the negativity, we often play little scenarios in our heads of all the things that could go wrong (or have gone wrong in the past), perhaps in the hope that this will prepare us better for the moments of danger. What we're actually doing is *rehearsing failure*.

Rehearsing failure is counterproductive. For a start, the more you rehearse failure, the better you will probably get at failing. Second, the more of these bad scenarios you run, the more stressed you'll probably feel. When you're stressed, you can't learn, so you'll find it harder to change your behaviour.

If you *must* run mental movies of things going wrong, at least use a detached viewpoint. Imagine looking at a video of yourself behaving in this way, on a television screen. Imagine slowing the video down; carefully examine your behaviour and assess what you could do differently. 'Reframing' in this way tends to remove the emotional charge from your mental scenario.

Of course, a much better option than rehearsing failure is to rehearse success. This is not 'positive thinking'; it is running scenarios in our heads, in a carefully disciplined way, of ourselves behaving successfully.

Rehearsing success

1 Make yourself comfortable, in a quiet room, and close your eyes. Remove all distractions. (With a bit of practice, you'll find yourself being able to do this exercise just about anywhere. Be kind to yourself to start with.)

2 Imagine a television set. Set it down across the room and switch it on.

3 On the television screen, run a video of yourself performing well at a networking meeting. Watch the video carefully and notice what 'you' are doing. You can decide what you're watching; modify your imagined performance until you feel good (eager, excited or inspired).

4 Now adjust the video to make it really compelling. Turn up the sound; increase the screen size. Many people find that making it life-size, full colour, 3D, with surround-sound, works best.

5 Now, step into the movie so you are seeing the action through your own eyes, as if you were already there. Become aware of what you are *doing*, how you *look*, how you *sound* and how you *feel*.

6 Now step out again and shift your viewpoint a little way into the future beyond the event. Now you're looking

back on it, taking notes and thinking about what you did well. Notice how you feel about it now.

7 Come back to now. Freeze-frame the video at a point where you can easily remember the image. That image will be your access point into the video, so that you can re-run it whenever you want.

Identifying goals

Now that you have prepared yourself, you need to set yourself clear goals for the networking event. Why are you attending, specifically? To make new friends? To look for new ideas? To create new relationships that might become new customers?

Working out your own goals

It's useful to think of your goals in terms of what you want, and what you want to give. Answer these questions carefully; write down your answers.

What do I want to gain? What do I want to give?

Make your answers positive. The answers should motivate you towards, not away from something.

How will I know when I have gained it? How will I know when I have given it?

Write down specifically the evidence telling you that you have achieved your goal. What information will you have? What promises will you have made, or secured?

Is my goal truly mine?

Have you chosen this goal? Is it something that you have initiated? Sometimes we are set goals by our managers. If so, make sure you're happy with what you're being asked to achieve; negotiate if necessary, so that you feel in control of your goals. Be careful, also, to set only your own goals. We sometimes set goals for others: 'I want Peter to offer me a place in his team'; 'I want Marilyn to accept my offer of project support'. Concentrate on your own behaviour, not on others' actions.

What's the context?

Where will this goal take you? How does the goal for your networking event relate to your values, your strategy and your 'brand'? Are you willing to take on the responsibility that achieving the goal will give you? To give up what you might have to sacrifice to make the goal happen? Are you comfortable with this goal?

THE SKILLS OF NETWORKING CONVERSATIONS

However much you prepare, the moment comes when you have to get going. You have to walk into the room and start talking to somebody.

There is no one way of doing this. Some people can't resist starting with a humorous remark; others use well-established lines like: 'Have we met before?' or 'What brings you here?' The important thing is that you do it. Make contact.

Establishing rapport

Look back at the notes on building rapport in Chapter 1. Start positive or neutral. Complaining about the food is one way to make contact, but before long you may find yourselves agreeing that everything about the occasion is disastrous. Avoid emotive subjects such as religion and politics – at least to start with – and be very careful about assumptions linking one person with another. 'Are you married?' can be an embarrassing opener – as I found to my cost a few nights before writing this chapter.

Be appropriately vulnerable. The other person may well be feeling as nervous as you are; acknowledging your own apprehensions – especially if you go first – actually expresses confidence and is an excellent free gift with which to start the conversation.

It's more than likely that you won't remember the person's name within the first few minutes of your conversation. Too much else will be going on. A few simple tricks will help a name to stick.

- *Use their name* on first introductions.
  Hi, I'm Megan.
  Megan, hi. Pleased to meet you. I'm Tony.
- *Ask for the name again if necessary.* Taking the trouble to ask is another gift that will be appreciated.
- *Use the other person's name once or twice during the conversation.* Some people tend to be better at doing this than others; in my experience, Americans are more adept than Europeans at dropping your name into the conversation. It might feel a little awkward or false, but it will help you remember the name.

Keeping the conversation going

In the early stages of a conversation, try to listen more than speaking. Be the first to ask a question; then listen to the answer. Make sure that it's an open question, beginning with one of the six 'w's.

What do you do for a living?

Where do you meet most of your clients?

When did you start on this line of business?

Who is your link with the host organization?

How did you start out?

Be careful with the question 'Why?' It's hard not to sound like an interrogator using that word, however hard you try.

Now listen for remarks that will generate another question. Have that question ready in the back of your mind as you listen on: you've solved the next move in the conversation and can relax a little!

Share something about yourself. (Remember the rule in Chapter 1: no more than three questions before you make a different kind of move.) Try to link your remark to what the other person has said. If you feel comfortable, shift the conversation to start discussing your aims for being there – and perhaps your aims for this conversation.

Summarize and paraphrase. Check your understanding of what the other person is saying; this keeps you focused, gives you time to think of something else to say and shows that you're listening.

Another way to keep the conversation going is to bring someone else in.

Chris, come and join us. We're just talking about...

I know who you should meet. Let me try to find Firoze...

'Passing the ball' in this way can relax or enhance a conversation. It can also be a good way to bring a conversation to a close politely: having introduced people to each other, you can excuse yourself and move on.

Joining groups

Approaching a group of people is slightly different from approaching an individual. People often worry about how to break into group conversations that are already in progress – and whether to do it. Being able to 'read' the group is helpful.

- *Arrive early*. One of the best ways to manage groups is to be in at the start of one.
- *Use previous contacts*. Everyone you speak to early in the event is a potential 'joiner' later: use one as a link person if you want to join a group.
- *Judge the tightness of the group*. How closely are people standing to each other? How is their eye contact? Can you see an opening, or is the group broadcasting its exclusivity by turning all backs on the rest of the room?
- *Exploit fractures*. Conversations rarely survive being extended beyond three people. Groups of four or more will either be

audiences, listening to a single, dominant person, or mini-groups in the process of splintering from the main group. You could join the audience; or you could look for two people talking and gently insinuate yourself as a third.

- *Pick off stragglers.* Not everyone in the group will be entirely 'in the circle'. Find someone at the edge – perhaps they're looking as if they want an excuse to move on – and approach them.

- *Use listening time to establish your presence.* Make eye contact; respond to what someone is saying with smiles and nods. Ask a question as your first contribution: it's a good way to enter a conversation without being too rude.

- *Ask permission.* Find different ways of asking permission to enter new space.

> *Excuse me, I don't mean to interrupt, but I overheard you talking about...*

> *Forgive me for interrupting, but am I right in thinking that...?*

> *Sorry to barge in, but can I just ask you about what you were saying?*

'Playing host' is a brilliant way to break into groups. Pick up a bottle of wine or a plate of nibbles and circulate. Playing host is also a great way to build rapport. You're putting people at their ease; you're offering gifts (always a great way to get people interested in you); you're able to introduce people to each other. Playing host also helps *you*: it gives you a certain authority (or at least something to do), and it gives you control. You can judge when to stay with someone and when to move on.

> ### Pick someone who is alone!
>
> One way to deal with the problem of breaking into groups is to start your own. Look out for someone who is on their own and looking uncomfortable. Approach them kindly and gently; share your own vulnerability. Use the occasion to exercise all your conversation skills. Draw in other people; introduce your new contact to someone you already know. Before you know it, you'll be the centre of a brilliant group conversation.

Closing the conversation

Whether the conversation has gone well, or not gone anywhere in particular, take care to close it well. The final impression we make is almost as important as the first one.

Never leave someone abruptly. A simple way to exit from a conversation is to connect the person to someone else in the room. Make the introduction; make sure that it has stuck (are they actually exchanging more than one remark with each other?); and walk away. Alternatively, use a plausible reason for leaving. Maybe you're expecting a colleague to arrive; maybe there's someone you need to speak to before they leave.

These are simple strategies for closing a conversation. But think a bit more deeply before you use them.

In Chapter 3, we looked at the WASP structure of conversation: *w*elcome, *a*cquire, *s*upply, *p*art. Make sure that the conversation covers every stage before moving on. What can you supply? Have you promoted yourself and your work clearly? What are the other person's needs? Ask: 'How can I help them?', 'Who do I know that might be of interest to them?'

Explore possibilities and opportunities. How could this person help you? Don't be afraid to share your needs and goals. Doors might open in the conversation that neither of you had previously noticed. The question 'Who do you know who…?' can be a powerful networking question. You're networking to ask, not to demand. Even if they look like a good prospect, don't sell.

The parting stage of a conversation should always involve action of some sort. Lots of actions could end a conversation. You could:

- invite the person to meet someone else;
- make a gift of information (or food, or drink…);
- agree to meet again;
- exchange cards.

Exchanging cards

The etiquette of exchanging business cards has become more sophisticated in recent years. Business cards are gifts; treat them as such and you won't go far wrong.

Keep your cards in good condition. This applies to cards you receive as well as your own. Business cardholders are a good idea; one for your own, one for cards offered. If someone gave you a gift, would you immediately stuff it away in your pocket?

Give your card respectfully. Choose who you offer your card to. Give your card when it's asked for; asking for a card is a compliment, so treat it as such. Ask permission to offer your card. If you give your card with respect, you'll instil respect for yourself. Above all, don't leave a pile of cards on a table.

Receive cards with respect. The person offering is also paying a compliment, by trusting you with their contact details. Treat the card as a gift. Take it carefully; look at it; read it (aloud, perhaps); offer a compliment or a positive comment ('What an interesting design'; 'Ah, I see you're based in London'). Put the card away respectfully, perhaps only after you have parted.

It's a good idea to make notes on business cards: where you met, who introduced you, interesting information, agreed follow-up actions. However, you should never write on a business card in the other person's presence. (Unless they give you permission to do so, of course.)

The international etiquette of business cards

People are increasingly aware that business cards are handled differently in different cultures. One website offers the following advice.

Middle East

Always present your card with your right hand, never your left.

China

Have one side of your business card translated into Chinese and in gold-coloured lettering, as that is considered auspicious. If your company has been established for a very long time, it's useful to state the year it was formed on the card. When offering the card, you should do so with both hands.

Japan

To give and receive business cards in Japan is quite ceremonial. Status is important in Japan so make sure your title is prominent on the card. And, whilst it's perfectly acceptable to give your card with one hand, make sure you accept one with both hands. Keep it on the table in front of you. If you're meeting several people at once who have all given you their cards, keep all the cards on the table in front of you until the meeting has concluded. Place them in front of you in the order in which people are seated, to help you remember their names.

India

Business in India places a great emphasis on academic achievement. Your business cards should state any university qualifications you have, or any other kind of honour. As in the Middle East, always use your right hand when offering a business card.
(http://www.worketiquette.co.uk/business-card-etiquette-in-various-countries.html)

FOLLOWING UP AND BUILDING YOUR NETWORK

Don't waste the opportunities you've worked so hard for. Once you've made contact with people, think about how you can make use of that contact. Review your cards and notes at the end of the event. Record in your diary any obvious or immediate plans for follow-up. Don't let the cards gather dust in your case!

Recording contacts

Find a way of organizing your network contacts. Whether on card or electronic, your system must allow you to find contact details with a minimum of fuss. It should also be easy to review and adjust. If you can align your system to other systems you use for personal details – your personal organizer, your e-mail archives – so much the better.

Re-connecting with people

Having the contacts is of little use if you don't use them. There are lots of ways of re-connecting to people you have met.

Follow up fast. Send an e-mail within 24 hours. This is common courtesy and also establishes you on their e-mail system. Make the e-mail personal; no round robins and no copying in.

Include a gift. Pick up on the conversation you were holding and offer anything that you think might be of interest. Typically, this will be more information: documents (brochures, e-newsletters), links or contact details for other people.

Invite them to make contact. It might be lunch; or a phone call; or another event where you could meet on neutral ground.

Avoid fatigue and annoyance. If someone doesn't reply, manage future contacts with care. Plan further 'nudges' over a period of weeks or months.

Asking for help

A very good way to re-connect is to ask for help. If there's something that the contact can do to assist you, invite them to offer it. It's flattering to be asked to give something. Make sure that you balance your requests with regular offers. (See the notes on the 'Netbank', below.)

'Joining the dots'

One of the most valuable gifts we can offer in business is contacts with other people. Generosity tends to beget generosity.

The general rule is to be carefully generous. Offer safe contact details: an e-mail address should be sufficient. If you're uncertain, check with the third person that they're happy to have their details passed on.

Constructing a network map

You could go further. Constructing a map of your network (or networks!) might help you get more value from them. In particular, they can help you find cross-connections between people in different parts of your life.

You could create network maps on paper, or using software such as MindManager or The Brain. With yourself at the hub of the map, draw links to various categories: 'Family', 'Community', 'Education', 'Work', 'Music', 'Clubs', 'Friends', and so on. Now add individuals to those categories that you know personally: people you'd feel happy cold-calling on the phone. Add links to people that you know that *they* know, or people that you're weakly tied to in some way. You could begin to add notes, colour coding and other visual effects to develop patterns or clusters of contacts (MindManager has plenty of functions to help you).

The trick in creating this network map is to concentrate on the *weak* ties. People with strong ties to you will tend to share your interests, expertise and contacts. People with weak ties have access to new information, resources and people; they are the ones who will help you most to grow and enrich your network. (The sociologist Mark Granovetter coined the phrase 'the strength of weak ties' to capture this idea.)

Keeping the connections alive

Think of your network as an organism. It is alive, continually shape-shifting and adapting itself to your environment: your personal circumstances, your work patterns, your ambitions and desires. Like any organism, it needs to be healthy to survive and grow: it needs feeding, nurturing, exercise – and occasional pruning.

Review your network regularly: perhaps once a year. Check contact details and clean out the system; move people around; make new connections. Ask how you can enliven contacts that have 'gone to sleep' for a while; think about how new relationships can help you in new ways.

In particular, look for the 'connectors'. Connectors have what Prince Charles calls 'convening power'. These are people who can act as mediators or 'honest brokers', putting people in contact with each other for mutual benefit. Ask how a connector could help you fulfil a need, and what would be in it for them.

The Netbank

We have a 'net account' with everyone in our network. Just like a real bank account, our net accounts with people can be in credit or overdrawn. (Whenever we say 'I'm in your debt', or 'I'm obliged', we are signalling the need to balance our net account with someone.)

Diane Darling suggests that the best way to check our net balance with someone is to try to make a withdrawal.

- When you need to call them, will you feel comfortable doing so?

- How long has it been since you put something into the account?
- The last time they asked you to help, did you do so?

If you think your net account with someone is dangerously low, make a deposit.

- Find something you can do for the person.
- Don't ask them for anything.
- Identify people with whom you are in 'net credit'. Could they help you with a 'net loan'?

Remember that deposits gather 'net interest'. A small deposit can quickly garner bigger returns.

Volunteering

Networking is a proactive business. Waiting for the phone to ring is not the way to do it. Get out there and exercise your communication skills; put yourself about; make yourself known.

Use your organization's facilities. Most organizations have employee networks, and social or activity-based groups that you can use to make new friends and useful contacts. Be guided by your interests, and network from your centre. Avoid whatever seems superficial or uncomfortable.

Start your own network. If an area of interest or a constituency seems under-represented in your organization, start a new network. Think about who might help you run it; look for sponsorship at senior levels; promote the network boldly. It's important that networks should not be seen as divisive or exclusive. The whole point is to bring people together, not drive them apart.

Organize a networking event. If you are responsible for setting up an event where people will be networking, you can do a great deal to make it easier for people to meet.

Volunteer. Put yourself forward to speak at meetings or conferences. Offer to chair meetings and to join committees. Become an author: editors of newsletters and magazines are often desperate for new providers of copy.

Cross boundaries. Look beyond your organization, to cross-industry organizations, and groups with shared intellectual or professional interests. Look at your network map and think about organizations linked to people you know – and to your weak ties, in particular.

Speed-networking: a proposal

Erica Munro is a writer who understands the necessity of networking while hating the word. In an amusing article on her website, she suggests a simple way to make networking palatable. It's designed along the speed-dating principle and it would go like this:

1 The word 'networking' would be banned.

2 So would warm white wine.

3 Also out – any suggestion that it's a social event. This is business. It would take place during the day, for a start, so as not to cut into precious evening time with family and friends.

4 The event would be split in two. First, everyone takes a number, a notebook and a pen.

5 Then everyone takes their turn to stand up and say who they are, what they do and what information they're looking to get out of the event. About 40 seconds each should do it.

6 The others all make notes.

7 When everyone is finished, participants head for the person or people who may be of use to them.

At last, it's speed-networking time. Name, rank, serial number, business card – all exchanged within a five-minute slot, with a little bell denoting when it's time to shake hands and move on.

Exploring

Effective networkers go sideways. They use every opportunity to practise their networking skills and seek new relationships.

Don't have a goal. Displaying a sense of purpose when networking usually kills it stone dead. Effective networking is about giving with no thought of any return. If you get nothing out of it, move on. But on most occasions, giving *does* give you a return.

Use the 'three-foot rule'. Everyone within a metre of you is potentially a conversation partner. This is because they are entering what Edward T Hall calls our 'personal space': the space we usually reserve for our friends. Go through a day noticing who comes into your personal space. Be ready to make eye contact and to say 'hello'. Find the friendly remark that might trigger conversation. Don't force people to talk to you, or put them under any obligation to you. Give, and see what happens. Notice what works and move on.

Trains and planes

Some of our most memorable conversations can be with strangers when travelling. Something about the neutral space of an airport or railway station makes it easier for us to reach out to people. Here are some tips on making the most of travelling time.

Carry a book or a music player. This shows that you are not desperate to talk – and offers an escape route if the person turns out to be difficult or boring. A book can also be a conversation starter.

When you sit down near another person, smile and greet them. Notice their response.

Respect the other person's personal space – especially when it is constricted (particularly important on aircraft!).

Offer help – luggage, directions, useful information. This is a great way to break the ice. But don't expect anything in return!

Observe body language. If the person isn't interested in talking, their body will tell you so.

Show interest. Ask a question and show appreciation of the answer. We all love to feel that we have taught someone something!

Find new ways of making your voice heard. People now keep in touch in a host of ways: social networking sites, e-mail, instant messaging, blogging... Think about how you can use electronic media to promote your messages and offer useful gifts to people in your network.

Use some simple disciplines to nudge your thinking into new areas. This is not a matter of simply, 'thinking outside the box'. Deliberately ask key questions, such as:

- How else could I view this relationship?
- How do they see me?
- What don't they know about me?
- Who else would be interested in this?
- How else could I present this idea?
- Where else would this work?
- What would this look like in a completely different business sector?

We often need help simply seeing our situation in fresh ways. Who are the trusted friends in your network who could help you get a fresh perspective?

What really interests you? What is your intuition telling you? If you don't act on your hunches, you'll never know whether there was something there.

The 10 commandments of effective networking

1 You get what you give.

2 Be yourself.

3 Honour your relationships.

4 Share; don't hoard.

5 Ask for what you want.

6 Promote yourself professionally.

7 Move on when necessary.

8 Record all your contacts.

9 Follow up.

10 Expand your horizons.

In brief

- Networking is the art of building and sustaining mutually beneficial relationships.
- Networking is *not*:
  - selling;
  - using other people for your own gain; or
  - putting people on the spot.
- What makes networking effective
  - an abundance mentality
  - generosity
  - reciprocity
- Prepare to network by:
  - preparing yourself
  - building your brand
  - finding your core values
  - listing your achievements and accomplishments
  - creating a self-introduction
  - marshalling your resources
    - visual
    - vocal
    - verbal
- Your business card should:
  - reflect your brand
  - be easy to read
  - be of high quality
- Look after your inner self
  - Build up your confidence
  - Rehearse success
  - Identify your goals

- In the networking conversation:
  - establish rapport
  - use techniques to keep the conversation going
  - practise joining groups
  - close the conversation respectfully
  - use good etiquette for exchanging cards
- To follow up and build your network
  - record your contacts
  - re-connect with people
  - ask for help
  - create a network map
  - keep the connections alive
  - volunteer
  - use your organization's facilities
  - start your own network
  - explore
  - find new ways of making your voice heard
- The ten commandments of effective networking
  - You get what you give.
  - Be yourself.
  - Honour your relationships.
  - Share; don't hoard.
  - Ask for what you want.
  - Promote yourself professionally.
  - Move on when necessary.
  - Record all your contacts.
  - Follow up.
  - Expand your horizons.

APPENDIX WHERE TO GO FROM HERE

Communication is continuous, and we never finish learning how to improve. My blog explores issues and events relating to the material in this book. You can find it at: http://justwriteonline. typepad.com/distributed_intelligence. Here are some thoughts about books and other resources that will take further the ideas we have explored in this book.

CHAPTER 1: WHAT IS COMMUNICATION?

The fullest explanation I have found of the Shannon–Weaver model of communication is on Mick Underwood's magnificent (and award-winning) website: http://www.cultsock.ndirect.co.uk/ index2.html.

I also found David Chandler's page useful: http://www.aber. ac.uk/media/Documents/short/trans.html#N.

The four principles of communication are based on ideas by Donnell King. Find them at: http://www.pstcc.edu/facstaff/dking/ interpr.htm.

Steven Mithen's book *The Prehistory of the Mind* (Phoenix, London, 1998) discusses the origins of communication in primate activity. Margaret Wheatley's *Leadership and the New Science* (Berret-Koehler, San Francisco, 1992) brings insights from quantum theory and complexity to bear on ideas of information.

CHAPTER 2: HOW CONVERSATIONS WORK

Peter Senge's book *The Fifth Discipline* (Random House, London, 2nd edn, 2006) relates conversation to systems theory. William Isaac's *Dialogue and the Art of Thinking Together* (Currency Books, New York, 1999) is at the leading edge of studies into conversation.

CHAPTER 3: SEVEN WAYS TO IMPROVE YOUR CONVERSATIONS

First- and second-stage thinking are notions that inform Edward de Bono's work. Look at *Lateral Thinking in Management* (Penguin, London, 1982). The four types of conversation derive from the work of Michael Wallacek, who may have been influenced by Werner Erhard.

Chris Argyris' Ladder of Inference is best found in *The Fifth Discipline Fieldbook*, edited by Peter Senge and others (Nicholas Brealey, London, 1994).

For more on mindmaps, see Tony Buzan's *Use your Head* (BBC, London, 1974).

CHAPTER 4: THE SKILLS OF ENQUIRY

Nancy Kline's *Time to Think* (Ward Lock, London, 1999) is a fascinating study of deep listening.

CHAPTER 5: THE SKILLS OF PERSUASION

Peter Thompson's *Persuading Aristotle* (Kogan Page, London, 1999) relates classical rhetoric to modern business techniques entertainingly. For more on pyramids, look at Barbara Minto's *The Pyramid Principle* (Pitman, London, 1987).

CHAPTER 6: MAKING A PRESENTATION

Max Atkinson's book *Lend Me Your Ears* (Vermilion, London, 2004) takes a strikingly new approach to the subject of presenting and speech-writing.

CHAPTER 7: PUTTING IT IN WRITING

Alan Barker's *Writing at Work* (Industrial Society, London, 1999) is a comprehensive guide to writing business documents.

CHAPTER 8: NETWORKING: THE NEW CONVERSATION

Two books taking usefully complementary approaches to networking are Steven D'Souza's *Brilliant Networking* (Pearson Education, Harlow, 2008), and *Power Networking* by Donna Fisher and Sandy Vilas (Bard Press, Atlanta, USA, 2000).

Creating Success series

Dealing with Difficult People by Roy Lilley
Decision Making & Problem Solving by John Adair
Develop Your Assertiveness by Sue Bishop
Develop Your Leadership Skills by John Adair
Develop Your Presentation Skills by Theo Theobald
Effective NLP Skills by Richard Youell and Christina Youell
How to Deal with Stress by Stephen Palmer and Cary Cooper
How to Manage People by Michael Armstrong
How to Organize Yourself by John Caunt
How to Write a Business Plan by Brian Finch
How to Write a Marketing Plan by John Westwood
How to Write Reports & Proposals by Patrick Forsyth
Improve Your Communication Skills by Alan Barker
Successful Project Management by Trevor Young
Successful Time Management by Patrick Forsyth
Taking Minutes of Meetings by Joanna Gutmann

The above titles are available from all good bookshops.
For further information on these and other Kogan Page titles,
or to order online, visit the Kogan Page website at
www.koganpage.com